S0-DWF-927

Arms, Indians, and the Mismanagement of New Mexico

Donaciano Vigil

(Courtesy of the Historical Society of New Mexico Collection, Museum of New Mexico.)

Arms, Indians, and the Mismanagement of New Mexico

Donaciano Vigil, 1846

David J. Weber
Editor and Translator

Texas
Western
Press

The University of Texas at El Paso

Southwestern Studies Series No. 77

Copyright © 1986
Texas Western Press
The University of Texas at El Paso
El Paso, Texas 79968-0633

All rights reserved. No part of this book may be used or reproduced in
any manner without the written permission of Texas Western Press,
except in the case of brief quotations employed in reviews and similar
critical works.

First Edition
ISBN 0-87404-153-8 (paper)
ISBN 0-87404-156-2 (cloth)

Dedicated to my colleagues in the
History Department at SMU

Jeremy du Quesnay Adams	Glenn M. Linden
Kathryn Bernhardt	John Sherman Long
James O. Breeden	Luis Martín
Dennis D. Cordell	John A. Mears
Ronald L. Davis	Judy Jolley Mohraz
O. T. Hargrave	Donald L. Niewyk
Hans Hillerbrand	Daniel T. Orlovsky
James K. Hopkins	Jennifer Tolbert Roberts
Alphine Jefferson	R. Hal Williams

Whose remarkable collegiality
has made seven years as department chairman
seem half as long

Contents

Introduction

First-hand accounts of conditions in New Mexico in the years just before American troops invaded the province in August 1846 have come almost entirely from the pens of foreigners. Itinerant merchants and adventurers, such as Josiah Gregg, George W. Kendall, Alfred Waugh, James Josiah Webb, Lewis Garrard, and Adolph Wislizenus, wrote valuable book-length descriptions of New Mexico — then a Department of the Republic of Mexico.[1] Writing for an English-speaking audience unfamiliar with their subject, these outsiders displayed a keen interest in the details of daily life and in the province's leading personalities. Notwithstanding their biases and prejudices, these foreign visitors provided invaluable descriptions of New Mexico during its last years under independent Mexico. Hispanic New Mexicans, on the other hand, had few outlets for their prose and little need to record the commonplace or the obvious. In general, writing by *nuevomexicanos* of that day concerned itself with routine matters of business, law, and government; it rarely contained analysis or systematic commentary on the larger problems of the province. Among the few exceptions are two remarkable proposals by Donaciano Vigil, one of New Mexico's leading citizens.[2] Vigil directed his proposals to the New Mexico Assembly, but he hoped that they would be brought to the attention of federal officials in Mexico City. Published here for the first time in either English or Spanish, these proposals offer the perspective of a leading *nuevomexicano* on New Mexico's internal problems in June 1846, on the eve of the North American invasion.

From the vantage point of Mexico City or Washington, the outbreak of hostilities between Mexico and the United States was the paramount issue in June 1846. As seen from the remote provincial capital of Santa Fe, however, other issues loomed larger during the first days of that fateful summer. How would New Mexicans fill the perennially empty treasury and pay the salaries of government officials? How could New Mexicans defend themselves from neighboring tribes of hostile Indians? How could New Mexicans govern themselves effectively amidst Mexico's internal political convulsions?

New Mexico officials had known for many months that tensions were running high between the United States and Mexico. They had learned of the United States annexation of Texas and of the absurd Texan claims to the upper Rio Grande, including Santa Fe and Albuquerque. Reports had also reached Santa Fe of John Slidell's arrival in Mexico City in December 1845, and his attempt to purchase New Mexico and California for the United States. Indeed, some New Mexicans suspected that the central government in Mexico City would sell their Department to the *norteamericanos*. By early summer of 1846, word reached New Mexico that Slidell had failed to buy New Mexico, but that American forces had been sent to the mouth of the Rio Grande. The threat to New Mexico from what Governor Manuel Armijo termed "our neighbor, the giant," was clear.[3] By the end of June, however, with the United States invasion just six weeks away, New Mexico officials still did not know that the American president, James K. Polk, had declared war on Mexico on May 13, or that over 1,600 American troops had left Fort Leavenworth, Missouri, to march 800 miles to Santa Fe.[4] Donaciano Vigil, like other members of the small New Mexico oligarchy, had more pressing matters on his mind.

In June 1846, Donaciano Vigil submitted two proposals to the New Mexico Assembly. The first, read at a meeting on June 18, asked the five-member Assembly, of which Vigil was a *suplente*, or alternate member, to petition the Mexican Congress to allow guns and munitions to enter New Mexico free of all duties.[5] Increased firepower was vital to New Mexico's defense, but Indians rather than *norteamericanos* were the adversary from Vigil's point of view. His long written statement, which he may have worked on for over a month, described how the recent breakdown of relations between New Mexicans and neighboring tribes of "barbarians" had brought death and destruction to the province.[6] Behind the growing Indian belligerance, Vigil saw an American influence.

The coming of American merchants to New Mexico in the 1820s, Vigil explained, had brought better merchandise at lower prices than New Mexicans had previously known, but these merchants had also brought about a shift in the balance of power with potentially hostile tribes. Due in part to what Vigil believed to be harassment of foreigners by government officials, American merchants had moved their operations out of New Mexico's villages into American territory. On the high plains north of the Arkansas, which then served as the international boundary, the Americans built trading posts that soon came to dominate the Indian trade. This shift in control of the trade, from New Mexicans to Americans, Vigil argued, brought disaster to New Mexico. With guns obtained from the Americans, Indians thinned out the buffalo herds and sold the hides to Americans. This caused a shortage of wild game for New Mexicans. Even worse, Indians with American arms attacked New Mexico pastures and depleted the livestock. Vigil explained how local settlement patterns and grazing practices made New Mexico's sheep, horses, and cattle especially vulnerable to Indian depredations. Most tragically, however, Indians raiding New Mexico settlements took human captives, including women whom the "barbarians" brutalized.[7]

The picture Vigil painted was gloomy, but it was not new. New Mexicans had known since the 1820s that unscrupulous Americans, who traded guns and ammunition to Indians, provided Plains tribes with the means and motive to attack New Mexico settlements. The fullest exposition of the problem came from the pen of Antonio José Martínez, the vigorous parish priest of Taos. In a ten-page pamphlet, published at Taos in 1843 and directed to General Antonio López de Santa Anna, Martínez condemned the American traders.[8] To counter their influence he had proposed that the government "civilize" the "barbaric" Indians, teaching them to become self-sufficient on their own farms and ranches. Otherwise, as game disappeared, Indians desperate for food would destroy the farms and ranches of New Mexico.

Martínez's analysis of the problem contrasted with that of Donaciano Vigil. Whereas the nationalistic Martínez condemned the

Americans, Vigil suggested that misguided Mexican policies forced the Americans, whose enterprise he seemed to admire, to establish trading posts outside of Mexican territory. Whereas Martínez, the priest, sought peace through education, Vigil, who was a soldier, sought guns and ammunition to win a peace through war. Whereas Martínez hoped to involve the central government in efforts to pacify Indians, Vigil claimed that New Mexicans could no longer depend upon the central government and would have to solve the problem themselves.

Disillusioned with the frequent changes and political discord in the central government, Vigil made it plain that New Mexicans could not expect military aid from Mexico City. New Mexico's only recourse, Vigil believed, was to redress the balance of arms so that New Mexicans had the means to defend themselves. While hostile Indians enjoyed greater access to arms and munitions than ever before, some New Mexicans, especially those from the poorer class, were reduced to defending themselves with bows and arrows. New Mexicans could not obtain firearms or powder and shot, Vigil explained, because the government prohibited the import of guns and ammunition from abroad — that is, over the Santa Fe Trail from the United States.

Vigil proposed that the ban be lifted, allowing foreign weapons and munitions to enter New Mexico free of tariffs. If Vigil had taken seriously rumors of conflict with the United States, he might not have proposed this arrangement, which would make New Mexico dependent for arms on its soon-to-be adversary. But the shortage of arms, as Vigil saw it, was so severe that a couple of weeks after he made his proposal of June 18, when it appeared likely that American forces would invade New Mexico, Vigil counseled Governor Manuel Armijo against defense. How could New Mexicans resist with only "quivers and slings," Vigil asked rhetorically.[9]

Won over by its "solid reasons and justice," the New Mexico Assembly followed Vigil's recommendation to send copies of the proposal to Congress and to New Mexico's representative in Congress, Tomás Chávez y Castillo.[10] If copies of the proposal reached Mexico City, they arrived too late to help the besieged province. Although Vigil had not yet learned of it, fighting had already begun between Mexico and the United States. Mexico was at war, even as Vigil spoke.[11]

Four days after he addressed the Assembly on the subject of arms and munitions, Donaciano Vigil submitted another measure for the lawmakers' consideration. On June 22, Vigil asked the Assembly to petition the central government to stop filling the key posts of governor and commanding general of New Mexico with people who had no experience with local problems.[12] Vigil wanted those posts to go to men who were either natives of New Mexico or long-time residents. Since Vigil himself was a native of New Mexico and an office seeker, such a proposal might have been self-serving. Perhaps it was. As with his statement on arms and munitions, however, Vigil provided the Assembly with written arguments, drawing evidence from the events of recent years. In the process, he inadvertently left posterity a unique analysis of the last decade of Mexican administration of New Mexico.

In his proposal of June 22, Vigil examined the records of the three previous administrations, all headed by outsiders: governors Albino Pérez (1835-37) and Mariano Martínez (1843-45), and General Francisco García Conde (1845).

Governor Pérez, Vigil charged, failed to rely on local leaders, making them feel "snubbed." Pérez turned instead to "favorites," whom many people resented. Pérez led a military campaign against the Navajos, but knew nothing of Indian psychology. When the Navajos defeated him at the bargaining table, he lost the respect of those who had sacrificed much to fight in his ranks. Finally, Vigil charged, Pérez misread the condition of the local economy and tried to establish a system of direct taxation. A bloody revolt followed, in which Pérez and other officials were brutally murdered.

Vigil's contention that Pérez "caused" the 1837 rebellion in New Mexico contrasts with the views of many of his contemporaries. In Mexico City, the prominent lawyer, politician, and historian Carlos María Bustamante, had blamed the revolt on American merchants. Americans, Bustamante argued in a book published in 1842, had stirred up a revolt in order to avoid paying tariffs. In the aftermath of the Texas Revolt of 1836, Bustamante's position was understandable. He feared, quite correctly, that New Mexico, like Texas, would be lost. The Americans, Bustamante asserted, wanted to add still another "new star to the flag of Washington, deceiving those people [the New Mexicans], who have never been more free and independent than they are today, with joyful theories of liberty and independence."[13] Vigil, who had apparently read Bustamante's work, explicitly disavowed his interpretation.

Closer to home, some of Vigil's contemporaries in New Mexico blamed the 1837 revolt on the lower class, characterized by Governor Manuel Armijo as having "no other goal . . . than killing and robbing."[14] Vigil, on the other hand, seems to have sympathized and cooperated with the rebels, who had captured him and spared his life. In fact, Vigil had served as secretary for the semi-literate rebel leader, José Gonzales, and this had led to an investigation of Vigil's loyalty.[15]

Vigil put the responsibility for the 1837 revolt squarely on Governor Pérez and on the governor's upper class enemies. The latter, according to Vigil, took advantage of Pérez's mistakes to turn people against him. Since Vigil advanced this argument in a polemic against the appointment of outsiders to the governorship of New Mexico, his blaming of an outsider for the revolt may seem too convenient. Nonetheless, Vigil continued to argue that point of view even after it ceased to serve such an obvious purpose.[16]

Following the tragic demise of Pérez, Vigil noted, a native-born New Mexican, Manuel Armijo, served admirably as governor before another outsider, Gen. Mariano Martínez, arrived in 1843 to mismanage local affairs. Martínez, who came to New Mexico as commanding general, then assumed the governorship in May 1844, took a condescending view toward the *nuevomexicanos* and surrounded himself with sycophants, Vigil charged. Like Pérez, Martínez did not understand how to deal with Indians. He touched off a bloody war with the Utes, who had been at peace with New Mexico, as Vigil put it, "since time immemorial." Martínez also squandered departmental finances, failed to pay the troops, and extracted loans from the citizenry. Vigil suggests that New Mexicans were on the verge of another rebellion when Martínez left office on May 1, 1845.[17]

Vigil aimed the final salvo in his address of June 22 against Gen. Francisco García Conde, who had come to New Mexico on a brief tour of inspection in August 1845. Although he was only forty-one years old at the time of his visit to New Mexico, García Conde had already served as governor of two frontier states, Chihuahua and Coahuila, and as a member of Congress from his native state of Sonora. Moreover, he had played an important role in organizing the defense of northern Mexico against Apaches and Texans.[18]

By Vigil's definition, García Conde was an outsider to New Mexico, but few Mexican officers understood the plight of the frontier better than he. Nonetheless, García Conde's arrival in New Mexico, as Commanding General of the Fifth Division of the Mexican Army, coincided with a change in the military structure that may have prejudiced some New Mexico officers, such as Vigil, against him. With the arrival of García Conde in Santa Fe in mid-August 1845, the title of New Mexico's ranking military officer was reduced from *comandante* general to *comandante principal*. This made New Mexico's leading officer subordinate to the *comandante general* in Chihuahua — García Conde. New Mexicans had resented this arrangement when it existed earlier, for they felt that it limited their ability to make quick decisions locally. New Mexico officers probably bristled when they were again made subordinate to Chihuahua in 1845.[19]

Whatever García Conde might have accomplished on his tour of New Mexico, all that Vigil recalled was negative. García Conde made a foolish military appointment, Vigil claimed, which alienated New Mexico's officers. He overextended his authority by confiscating funds from the treasury, and by firing local treasury officials unfairly. Vigil says nothing about García Conde's negotiations with the Comanches, which appears to have been one of the principal reasons for his long journey to New Mexico.[20]

Vigil concluded his second proposal to the Assembly just as he had the first. He asked that New Mexico's representative to Congress, Tomás Chávez y Castillo, be instructed to seek a measure that would assure that the chief military and civil offices of New Mexico "always be given to people who have lived long enough among us to know our true interests intimately." This time, the Assembly did not move quickly to endorse Vigil's proposal. Instead, the deputies agreed to follow the usual procedure of reading the measure at two subsequent meetings of the Assembly prior to taking a vote.[21]

Opposition to the proposal apparently existed, for on June 29, when it was scheduled to be read for the second time, Vigil asked that the reading be postponed until the next day to give him time to make additional comments and to add proper punctuation. At this juncture, news of the imminent invasion from the United States reached Santa Fe and pushed aside other business of the Assembly. On July 6, Vigil's proposal returned to the floor for a second reading. After hearing it on this occasion, the deputies decided not to have the measure read again, but to return it to Vigil and ask him to modify it, reducing it to its essential arguments and omitting phrases that might injure any authority or public body. Vigil was apparently absent from this meeting. He never resubmitted the proposal. Events later that summer would have made the exercise meaningless.[22]

The author of the proposals of June 18 and June 22 was an active participant in the public affairs that he described. An educated member of the family of a minor public official, Donaciano Vigil was an ambitious army officer and holder of public office. Like many of his contemporaries on the Mexican frontier, he has not been the subject of a good biography, but the general outline of his career is known.[23]

Born in Santa Fe on September 6, 1802, Vigil received an unusually good education for a frontiersman. His father, Juan Cristóbal Vigil, reportedly educated his sons at home. As one merchant later recalled, Donaciano and his brother Juan were widely known as "among the best educated men in public life in the department."[24]

Following the example of his father, whose early years were spent as a career soldier in Santa Fe, Donaciano Vigil entered the military in 1823 as a private, fighting in an arduous campaign against the Navajos that year. The military life must have suited him, for he made it a career. Vigil's physique seemed to have preordained him for military life. In his early twenties he was said to stand six feet, five inches tall, to weigh 220 pounds, and to possess enormous strength. Promoted to sergeant in 1832, Vigil came to head the San Miguel del Bado Company, headquartered at Santa Fe. He fought in numerous campaigns against Indians, joined with government forces in the futile attempt to contain the tragic rebellion against Governor Pérez in 1837, and participated in the successful routing of an invading force from Texas in 1841. The latter won him promotion to lieutenant and then to captain.

But Vigil was an unusual soldier in frontier New Mexico. His intelligence and training opened doors for him that would have been closed to an ordinary soldier. He held such posts as army supply clerk, secretary to the rebel Governor Gonzales in 1837, and secretary to Governor Manuel Armijo in the early 1840s. On two occasions, 1838-40 and 1843-45, Vigil served as a regular member of the Department Assembly, occasionally holding the post of secretary for that body. In 1846, when he prepared the two proposals translated here, he served as an "alternate" member of the Assembly. In addition to holding public offices, the soldier Vigil also published a newspaper, *La Verdad*, which made its first appearance on February 8, 1844, under the auspices of the maligned Governor Martínez and continued to appear for over a year. To augment his modest and undependable soldier's salary, Vigil was shrewd enough to get into the lucrative Santa Fe mercantile trade. In that business, he apparently came to know many Americans.[25]

In the summer of 1846, although he knew that resistance might be futile, Vigil joined in preparations for defense against the invading American army. Like other New Mexico soldiers, Vigil appears to have been surprised by Governor Manuel Armijo's last-minute decision not to oppose the entrance of American forces into Santa Fe.

With the American conquest of New Mexico, Vigil came into his own as a politician and landowner. After Stephen Watts Kearny secured Santa Fe, Vigil resigned his commission in the Mexican army and on September 22, 1846, received an appointment to the key office of the secretary of the first civilian government established by the United States in New Mexico.[26] Kearny had sought to fill a high post in the new government with a *nuevomexicano*, and Vigil probably received the appointment because of his knowledge of English and his friendship with influential Americans.

At the same time that he cooperated with the American occupying forces, the pragmatic Vigil maintained his loyalty to Mexico. On September 26, four days after his appointment as territorial secretary was announced, Vigil signed his name to a lengthy letter to the president of Mexico. Vigil and other prominent New Mexicans who signed this letter blamed Governor Manuel Armijo for their failure to fight the Americans. With proper leadership, they explained, "we would have made some kind of resistance."[27] Armijo, whose leadership Vigil had praised when he addressed the Assembly on June 22, now became the scapegoat.

The bloody rebellion against the American occupying forces that exploded in Taos in January 1847 not only took the life of Governor Charles Bent, another Kearny appointee, but it also catapulted Vigil into prominence. As the second-ranking civilian office holder in the territory, Vigil assumed the position of acting governor after Bent's death. Pragmatically, Vigil urged his fellow citizens not to resist. The fate of New Mexico had not yet been decided, Vigil explained, because Mexico and the United States had not signed a treaty of peace. But whether New Mexico became part of the United States or was returned to Mexico, Vigil asked his countrymen, would it not be "a gross absurdity to foment rancorous feelings toward people with whom we are either to compose one family, or to continue our commercial relations?"[28]

After American forces crushed the rebellion, Vigil offered his resignation as acting governor in order to pave the way for a new federal appointee, but the military command in New Mexico refused to accept his resignation. Vigil continued to serve as acting governor until December 1847, when he was appointed governor. With a de facto military government operating as "the power behind his every action," as one historian has put it, Vigil worked to strengthen civil government in New Mexico and to make New Mexico a territory of the United States.[29] He held the governorship until October 11, 1848, when Lt. Col. John M. Washington replaced him. Vigil was then reappointed Territorial Secretary, holding that office until March 1851 when the government was reorganized under the new constitution. He continued to hold public office, serving repeatedly in the territorial legislature until the end of the Civil War.[30] In his late sixties, in 1871-72, Vigil served a term as school commissioner of San Miguel County.

As a respected former governor and friend of influential Americans, Vigil used his knowledge of Mexican law and practice to make himself indispensable in matters involving land. Manipulating lawyers, documents, and finances with the moral abandon and skill of a Thomas Benton Catron or a Stephen Elkins, Vigil acquired a claim to two large ranches on the Pecos River in 1854.[31] The next year he moved his family from its home near the Church of Guadalupe in Santa Fe (a home that still stands today at 518 Alto Street) to the Pecos. The Vigil ranch, located in the midst of land that once belonged to Pecos Pueblo, would be Vigil's last home. A robust man in his old age, whose feats of strength had become the stuff of legends, he rode some twenty-five miles on horseback from Pecos to Santa Fe just a few months before his death in August 1877, at age seventy-four.

After his death, Vigil was eulogized as a man who loved liberty, who stood for governmental and social reforms, and who forcefully advocated the improvement of public education and clerical reform. He may have been, as historian Howard R. Lamar has put it, "one of the most unusual men to ever live in New Mexico."[32]

Donaciano Vigil's proposals to the New Mexico Assembly are published here for the first time, in both English and Spanish, lightly annotated, with annotations keyed to the translations. I have tried in my translations to preserve the spirit and flavor of Vigil's prose, but my principal aim is to achieve clarity and grace in English. In some respects, these two goals have proven to be mutually exclusive. Vigil did not write clearly or gracefully in Spanish. His prose does not lend itself to translation. His syntax and spelling, sometimes archaic and sometimes simply erroneous, is nearly unintelligible on occasion. Some words and phrases suggest different interpretations. Scholars, then, should check my translations against the originals.

In addition to providing a clearer sense of Vigil's meaning, the publication of the Spanish versions of Vigil's proposals in this volume may be a convenience to historians, anthropologists, and linguists who want to know the original words and expressions that a frontiersman such as Vigil employed. New Mexicans in 1846 had their own orthography, syntax, and vocabulary. What words did they use for Indians, for an Indian village, or for the act of scalping? What vocabulary did they employ to express political, economic, or military concepts?

Transcribing Vigil's proposals proved nearly as difficult as translating them. On occasion, either Vigil or the person who copied them made a slip of the pen. Some words are illegible, some words misspelled, and some words misused. Fortunately, two contemporary copies of each document exist, enabling us to answer some questions through comparison.

The transcriptions that appear in this volume are as faithful to the original as I could make them, for I sought to retain the flavor and structure of a mid-nineteenth century New Mexico document. I have not, then, added diacritical marks to words that ordinarily carry them if those marks were not present in the original document. Thanks to the imagination of Dale L. Walker, director of Texas Western Press, we have been able to set the type to simulate those abbreviations that appear in the original manuscript with a horizontal line above them. Those horizontal lines indicate that letters in the middle of a word have been omitted, and include such abbreviations as $d\overline{ros}$. (for *derechos*), $gob\overline{no}$. (for *gobierno*), and $ad\overline{mon}$. (for *administración*). Abbreviations that appear in the original manuscript with letters raised above the line (such as *departam.*^{to} for *departamento*, or *solem.*^{te} for *solamente*), have also been reproduced faithfully in this printed version. I have not cluttered the Spanish transcription with clarifications in square brackets, for it seems likely that anyone with a fair reading knowledge of Spanish will readily see the patterns: the writer combines some words that we do not combine today (such as *porla* for *por la*), often abbreviates the word *que* with the letter *q.*, and the word *porque* by writing *porq.*, and regards as interchangeable the letters *s* and *c*, *s* and *x*, *v* and *b*, *y* and *i*, and *y* and the double *l*. The letter *h* is occasionally omitted from words that require it in modern Spanish, such as *hostilizar*, and added to words that do not need it, such as *era* (rendered *hera*).

This book has been a long time in coming to fruition. Although I finished the translations seven years ago, the press of other commitments prevented me from completing the editing until 1983-84, when a research leave from Southern Methodist University provided me with free time. I am indebted to Charles Ray Stewart, a former graduate student at SMU, for rendering the initial transcription of each document. His work and mine was facilitated by rough transcriptions that Janet Lecompte, of Colorado Springs, had made for her own research and had graciously offered to us.[33] In 1977, I took Stewart's transcriptions with me to Madrid, where I lived during the winter and spring of that year. There, in a city that prides itself on the purity of its Castilian, I worked in the Biblioteca Benjamín Franklin to polish the transcriptions and translate into English the frontier Spanish of a one-time subject of Spain's far-flung empire. Donaciano Vigil would have been amazed.

David J. Weber
Southern Methodist University
Dallas, Texas
May 1984

I

Vigil on Arms, Munitions, Trade, North Americans, and "Barbaric" Indians

June 18, 1846[1]

Honorable Assembly

The misfortunes that afflict our Department every day with greater frequency have reduced it to a state of such insecurity that it cannot continue in this decadent condition much longer. Eventually, one day, residents who have survived repeated attacks by the barbaric Indians who surround us, will try to abandon their homes in some communities.

Speaking to an Assembly such as this, whose members, due to their virtues, patriotism, and talent, are those who merited the confidence of the people in order to lead them along the legal pathway of happiness, I do not believe it is necessary to mention, and even less to contemplate, the repeated misfortunes that have befallen New Mexico, especially since the administration of General Martínez.[2] Men lacking in public spirit have witnessed with horror the growing number of deaths that the barbarians[3] have inflicted on our countrymen, and the enormous number of livestock that they have stolen.[4] There are few weeks when we do not receive news of one of these mishaps, or the other, or the two together. In this lamentable state of affairs, it is rather natural that the perceptive man should reason and inquire into the causes that have brought such misery to the region. He should also investigate the means that might be used to guard against them. This is the subject that the humble subscriber proposes to present with timidity and diffidence to this Assembly in the following speech, directing his voice to so honorable a body as this Assembly truly is.

Gentlemen[5]

Our elderly citizens persist in representing us as having enjoyed security and peace in the era of Spanish government, due to the peculiar location of New Mexico, separated entirely from the rest of the world by deserts and extensive barren plains that only the roving tribes of Indians frequented.[6] But for this reason alone, New Mexico has been exposed from time to time to varying degrees of depredations by its numerous barbaric neighbors. In addition to this circumstance, consider that nearly all the villages of New Mexico lay along the banks of the Rio Grande or along the narrow bottomlands of its tributaries. The population is thus distributed over terrain exceeding 100 leagues in length with an insignificant width. This places nearly all the settlements on the borders. One can see, then, why the barbaric Indians find so many vulnerable places in New Mexico.

Another reason and powerful inducement for both peaceful and warlike heathens to plunder New Mexico is that the industry of the area is more directed to raising livestock, especially sheep that can be marketed in the interior [of Mexico],[7] than to agriculture or manufacturing. The latter is still unknown here, and agriculture only produces what the inhabitants consume, for there is no way to sell produce that exceeds the needs of the New Mexicans. Sheep breeders must maintain a number of horses for the different duties of their shepherds and the care of their sheep. Those horses excite the avarice of the heathen who are at war, those who value sheep, and even those heathens who do not value sheep and who are at peace. It is known through experience that a heathen seldom resists the temptation to steal horses — the more so when he thinks, or is convinced, that he can steal them with impunity.

Since livestock cannot be cared for except at considerable distances from the settlements, the enemies who lie in wait for the occasion to steal them do not find in New Mexico the obstacles that exist in other areas. This is due to the location [of New Mexico's village], as previously explained. In other regions, where villages are often found distributed at a distance around pastures, people travel between villages and thereby discover [Indian rustlers] before it is too late.

In regard to the murders that gentiles frequently commit (in addition to the reasons already indicated and those of war and pillage), those murders must be attributed to the fact that the only worthy way that a heathen can win respect and authority among his people is by the number of scalps that he has brought to his villages. Thus, all heathens always yearn to acquire such trophies, regardless of the method.

Prior to Independence, most barbarous tribes surrounding New Mexico had no other commerce than the barter that the New Mexicans allowed them. They were not provisioned with firearms. For nearly all their necessities they depended upon the aforementioned bartering and the generosity of the government that annually gave them gifts or rewards.[8] For this reason, it is not strange that only one company of presidial soldiers, properly under a superior system of discipline, well armed, mounted, and supported in everything, along with the customary aid of the citizenry, protected this area. The soldiers even punished the barbarians in their own villages. For this reason, too, our forefathers had the good fortune of defeating hordes of barbarians, although they themselves were few. Perhaps, also, in some ways these circumstances gave our venerable forefathers the glorious victories that they achieved on the expeditions of the *Arroyo de don Carlos* and of the *orejas del conejo*.[9] The superiority of arms, the exacting service of well-disciplined, well-paid and well-led troops, and the cooperation of as many citizenry as were named who blindly obeyed the established authorities, these, gentlemen, were the elements by which the New Mexicans of the time of the Spanish government made themselves respected or feared by all the barbaric tribes who knew them.[10] The New Mexicans had better arms and were also superior in the other requisites of war.

Then the Mexican nation proclaimed the glorious Independence that New Mexico seconded with such enthusiasm. We were swept up by agreeable theories and by patriotic discourses that then circulated among us. We expected to enter a new era of happiness, and this word and the word "liberty" were those that were most used and most repeated in those days. We saw everything, then, through rose-colored glasses.

The year in which independence of the nation was declared [1821], we saw arrive in this area, for the first time, merchants from the neighboring Republic. They supplied us with better merchandise than we had known until then, and they sold merchandise to us at incomparable prices — much lower than we had been accustomed to paying for goods of inferior quality. Since then a larger and more varied selection of merchandise has arrived and the spirit of mercantile enterprises has also spread among us.[11]

At once, companies were formed to trap beaver in the rivers of this Department. But since the central government had closed this industry to foreigners, the governor of the Department,[12] don Bartolomé Baca, with the intention of familiarizing us with this trade, took it upon himself to give permits to trap beaver to those parties who requested them if they consisted of an equal number of natives [New Mexicans] and foreigners.[13] These groups of hunters not only trapped beaver, but also traded with heathens who showed themselves to be friendly. For the two purposes of hunting and trading in Indian territory, so much enterprise and capital was employed that from Abiquiú alone, in a single year, 160 *quintales* of beaver [fur] was exported to the United States. Its value at that time amounted to no less than about one hundred thousand *pesos duros*.[14] One supposes that the different companies that went into business at Taos during the same era obtained proportionately the same returns. It is known that they spent fifty to sixty thousand *pesos* every year for preparations, chiefly on horses and provisions.

In short, everything indicated improvement and prosperity during the first years of Independence. But, this did not last long. The evil spirit soon busied itself in spoiling the well-being that was so fortunate for this area. Some gentlemen, although of good intentions but imbued with the doctrines of other centuries and of another type of government, worked with determination to reestablish a *closed and exclusive* system [of trade]. Others viewed with envy the advantages that they supposed should have come to them from the business and bustle that the foreigners brought to their own businesses (in which they employed many Mexicans), and secretly or publicly denounced the foreigners to the authorities as lawbreakers and usurpers of benefits that belonged exclusively to Mexicans.[15] By dint of persisting with this bad principle, they gained a hearing from the authorities who were intimidated by the accountability with which they were continuously threatened. For these reasons, don Bartolomé Baca was relieved from governing within a short time.[16] The foreign investors found themselves involved in lawsuits and difficulties to such an extent that finally, tired of the persecutions and the unfounded suspicions of their adversaries, and fearful for the security and soundness of their speculations in this area in the future, most went to the other side of our border [across the Arkansas River]. There they established more firms to trade with the heathen of those places.[17] Gradually the New Mexicans were excluded in a way from this trade, because they were not able to compete with the price of merchandise with those establishments that paid taxes to no one.

Before this occurred, all expeditions that traded with heathens had set out from the settlements of this Department. An immense number of buffalo hides, chamois, etc. entered New Mexico and were later transported elsewhere. Now, buffalo hides are seldom seen and the number of chamois etc. has diminished considerably. So the situation remains, due to ignorance or to the wickedness of some, depriving New Mexico of a trade that gave it profits and influence with the heathens and, at the same time, increased its trade with the interior of the Republic. From this point there began the decline that has so rapidly returned us to a level of importance and wealth that is far inferior to that which we had prior to Independence.

During the same era that saw, for the reasons I have just indicated, the ruin of New Mexico's trade and importance with the heathens, a spirit of excessive ambition or mania for public office began to appear among us. Unfortunately, we are still not free of it in our political affairs. Dazzled by their petty ambitions, few busied themselves with the true interests of the region. In fact, those who held positions that enabled them to live leisurely at the expense of the government were never questioned about their capacity to do their jobs.

In some ways, the lot of the heathens around New Mexico improved at the same time that ours worsened. Many Americans, persuaded by their own interests, established forts on the Platte, Arkansas, and Red rivers.[18] Through these forts, heathens have been supplied amply with as much as they might need, in exchange for furs. Thus, little by little, all the heathens forgot us and lost their affection for us. As soon as they became familiar with firearms and considered themselves well supplied with them, they no longer feared offending us. Since then, one also notes, the livestock and buffalo, which once abounded even on the common lands of our villages, have been progressively diminishing so quickly that now we have come to feel their scarcity or their complete disappearance in many areas. Now our hunters travel over 100 leagues in search of them — a long journey of four months. For the last two years there has not been enough meat to sustain them on their return trip without coming home empty-handed. Under these circumstances [of shortage of game] the barbarians, incited by necessity, attack us in order to save themselves.

The condition of most New Mexicans has not worsened compared to what it was in the era of the Spanish government. On the contrary, all men of good faith will admit that they are better off in many respects. But the means that in those days made them rich and invulnerable in their homes and invincible on the field of battle, now make them poor and defenseless.

Gentlemen: Most of the inhabitants of New Mexico, and especially those who are most exposed to attacks by barbarians, are armed only with bows and arrows and these are scarce because they do not have the means to buy more — not to mention guns and ammunition.[19] The central government of the nation, continually distracted and occupied with more general concerns, has not been able to provide us with the protection we need and that we have wanted for our security. The few troops that are in this Department are employed in this capital (which is the theater of all contests when there are any) in sustaining the authorities and in keeping order among the inhabitants. Due to their number and due to the deterioration of most of their equipment, even if the troops were free from this service [of keeping order in Santa Fe], they would not be able to defend more than the place where they live. The arrogance of our barbaric enemies requires us to defend our extensive borders with thousands of disciplined troops. These troops must be provisioned in the manner of the presidial system that was here in the era of the Spanish government — something that the National Treasury has not been able to do.

In any event, to wait for such protection from the central government of the nation would be to wait in vain. This is especially true given the degree to which the Republic has been weakened by the different [political] factions that are continually forming, as well as conflicting interests and unbridled ambitions. Thus, for our personal security and our interests (at least in regard to the barbarians), I believe we should not count on any protection or resources other than those the New Mexicans themselves can provide. But, so that the New Mexicans might display some new energy, we should obtain means of defense for them — arms and munitions. It is a calamity that we have always lacked these two very important items here. Although some of the wealthy class have acquired some luxurious guns from merchants who brought them for their own use, these cannot be obtained by most people. Nor is it the rich who usually go in pursuit of the barbarians when they have carried out a raid.[20] The introduction of arms and munitions is prohibited by our laws, and the government has no public arsenal here for either arms or ammunition.[21] Nonetheless, they are indispensable for us if we wish to exist in this Department. We are exposed to the same or worse horrors than those that occur in departments more populous and wealthy than ours, and that do not defend themselves well, no doubt due to some of the same problems we suffer here.

Gentlemen: I have heard reports regarding the barbaric tribes: of the number of Mexican captives, and especially of young Mexican women who serve the bestial pleasures of the barbaric Indians; of the brutal treatment they receive; and of the kinds of deaths that the barbarians are accustomed to inflicting for whatever capricious reason. Those reports have made me tremble with horror, have made me grieve, and have made me ashamed as I consider the degree to which bad luck has dogged our nation. The more so when I contemplate what the fate will be of many people whom I esteem, if timely measures are not taken to guard against such degrading misfortunes.

I do not doubt, gentlemen, that if the people of New Mexico could acquire arms and ammunition at reasonable prices, the same barbarians who now insult our defenseless situation will very quickly learn to respect us. Or, to put it better, to fear us. The heathen Indians have not improved their condition [since the Spanish era], neither physically nor morally. Their strength is only based on our accidental weakness.

Give the New Mexicans the means to acquire arms and inspire them with love of country. Then, moved by their interests, by their honor, and by the low prices of arms and their inclination to use them, I am confident, gentlemen, that the descendants of the ancient discoverers and conquerers of this immense continent will inflict ample punishment upon the barbarians if, to their own sorrow, they do not cease their present conduct toward us.

The quality and low prices of arms and munitions are achieved by the same means as that of any other article of merchandise — by free competition among those who sell them.

The Spanish race, gentlemen, has not degenerated in New Mexico, as is well attested to by some recent, if not impartial, deeds. The extent of our misfortune now makes all true New Mexicans[22] anxious for ways and means to aid our security and to prove to the nation and to the entire world that we, by our own virtues, are worthy in every way of the inheritance of our forefathers.

The Governor and Commanding General of the Department, don Manuel Armijo, fortunately has returned to direct our destinies. I am confident that he will not spare means or energy to guarantee our security and well being, just as he assured it in earlier times when resources were rather scarce, through his activity, prudence, experience, and good fortune.[23]

To obtain such desirable and happy goals, I propose to this Honorable Assembly that it should direct to the Supreme Congress of the nation a proposal based upon the arguments that I have just put forth, and the others that your excellencies consider appropriate. In order to free us as much as possible from the injuries that the barbarians cause us, and only while our critical circumstances last, we should ask Congress that it deign to decree that: the introduction of arms and munitions to the Department of New Mexico is permitted, free of all duties.

For the same purpose, I also propose that the Honorable Assembly send a copy of the previous proposal to our worthy representative in the Congress of the Union, don Tomás Chávez y Castillo, with a special recommendation that he support it and promote its speedy dispatch. Thus, if a favorable result is obtained, as is hoped, he may have news of it in the trading season, and this autumn or early next spring the means of securing our lives and our property might come to us.

Santa Fe
June 18, 1846
Donaciano Vigil [Signature]

II

Vigil opina sobre armas, municiones, comercio, norteamericanos, y indios bárbaros

18 Junio 1846

Honorable Asamblea

Las desgracias que cada dia con mas frecuencia afligen á nuestro Departam.^{to}, lo hán reducido á un estado tan poco seguro q. yá no podrá seguir mucho tiempo en este estado de decadencia sin que eventualmente algun dia, traten de abandonar sus recidencias en algunas poblaciones los havitantes q. sobrevivan álos repetidos ataques de los Yndios barvaros que lo circundan.

Hablando á una Asamblea como V.E. [Vuestra Excelencia] cuyos vocales son los que por sus virtudes, patriotismo y talento han merecido la confiansa del Pueblo para que lo dirija por la senda legal dela felicidad; no creo que sea necesario referir, y menos de ponderar las repetidas desgracias q. particularmente desde el tiempo de la admon. [administración] del Sōr. Grāl. [Señor General] Martinez á esta parte hán cabido al Nuevo Mejico. Los hombres de menos espiritu publico han visto con asombro el crecido numero de muertes q. los barvaros hán cometido en nuestros paisanos, y el cuantioso de ganados mayor y menor q. nos hán robado pues pocas son las semanas que no tenemos noticia de una ú otra desgracia, cuando no de las dos juntas. En este estado lastimoso de cosas es bastante natural q. el hombre sencible, rasone é inquiera, sobre las causas q. han acarreado al Pais tantas miserias, y tambien de indagar los medios que pudieran emplearse para precaverlas, este és el obgeto q. se propone haser presente á V.E. en el siguiente discurso el humilde subscritor que con timidés y desconfiansa, dirije su vóz á tan honorable Cuerpo como lo és verdaderam.^{te} V.E.

Señor

Aun en tiempo del Gobno. [Gobierno] Español q. nuestros ancianos compatriotas, se empeñan en representarnos como muy seguros y pacificos porla peculiar localidad del Nuevo Mejico, separado enteram.^{te} del resto del mundo, por desiertos y paramos dilatados q. solam.^{te} frecuentan las tribus de Yndios errantes, há sido en todo tiempo por sola esta rason, espuesto de cuando en cuando á mas ó menos depredaciones de sus numerosos barvaros vecinos; pero cuando concideramos q. á demas de esta circunstancia por estar casi todos los poblados del Nuevo Mejico sobre las marjenes del Rio del Norte ó sobre las angostas vegas de sus tributarios, y q. asi distribuida la poblacion en una largura de terreno de ciento y mas leguas, con un ancho incignificante, constituyen casi todas las poblaciones en frontera, entonces se vé porq. los indios barbaros hallan en el Nuevo Mejico tantos puntos bulnerables.

Otra causa y aliciente poderoso para q. los gentiles de páz ó de guerra cometan depredaciones en el Nuevo Mejico és, quela industria del pais se dirije mas bien ála cria de ganados particularm.^{te} menor (porq. tiene su espendió en el interior) que ála agricola ó fabril. Esta ultima no se conose aqui todabia, y la agricultura solo se estiende álo q. consumen sus havitantes, pues q. no hubiera salida para la q. ecsediera delo nesesario para los Nuevo Mejicos. Los criadores tienen q. mantener para los diferentes servicios de sus pastorias, y el cuidado de sus ganados, una porcion de caballada, la cual despierta la codicia, no solo delos gentiles q. estan de guerra, y delos q. aprecian los ganados, pero hasta la de los q. no los aprecian y de los q. estan de páz, pues se sabe por esperiencia q. rara vez reciste un gentil la tentacion de robar caballada, y mas cuando piensa, ó se combense q. la puede robar con impunidad; Y como los ganados no pueden cuidarse sino á largas distancias delos poblados, los enemigos que espian la ocacion de robarlos no encuentran en el Nuevo Mejico porlas rasones yá dhas. [dichas] respecto ála localidad, los obstaculos q. en otros paises donde los pastos se hayan muchas veces circulados álo lejos de poblaciones,

cuya gente por su intercurso entre si los hase descubrir en tiempo opor-
tuno. Por lo q. respecta álas muertes q. frecuentem.^{te} cometen los gentiles se deven atribuir á, ademas delas rasones yá indicadas, y álas de
guerra ó de robo, á q. el unico merito que a un gentil le procura concideracion y mando entre sus gentes, és el numero de cabelleras que há
llevado á sus rancherias, y por eso siempre ancian todos ellos por adquirir semejantes Trofeos, no importa como.

Antes dela Yndependencia las mas de las tribus varbaras q. circundan el Nuevo Mejico, no teniendo mas comercio que el trato — rescate
q. se permitio á estos havitantes con ellos, no estaban provistos de armas de fuego y dependian para casi todas sus nesecidades del dicho
rescate y dela generocidad del Gobierno enlos regalos ó gratificaciones
q. seles davan anualmente. Por eso no és estraño q. con solo una compañia de Precidiales bien que bajo un sistema sup.^r de disciplina, bien
armada, montada y asistida en todo, con el aucilio aconstumbrado de
los vecinos protegian este pais y aun llebavan el escarmiento álos varbaros hasta sus mismas rancherias. Por eso tambien tubieron nuestros
mayores la fortuna de vencer á muchedumbres de varbaros siendo ellos
pocos, y a caso tambien en cierto modo les deben nuestros benerables
mayores á estas mismas circunstancias, las gloriosas victorias q. conciguieron enlas jornadas del Arroyo de D. Carlos y el delas orejas del
conejo. La superioridad delas armas, el servicio ecsacto de una tropa
bien disciplinada, pagada, y mandada, y la cooperacion de cuantos
vecinos se nombraban, que obedecian entonces ciegamente álas
autoridades constituidas, esos fueron Señores, los elementos con q. los
Nuevo Mejicos del tiempo del Gobno. Español, se hicieran respetar ó
temer de todas las tribus barvaras q. los conocieron. Esto és porq. tenian mejores armas, y q. les heran tambien superiores en los demas requicitos para la guerra.

Luego q. se proclamó la gloriosa Yndepend.^a dela Nacion Mejicana,
que el Nuevo Mejico secundó con tanto entuciasmo llebados de las
lisongeras teorias; y delos discursos patrioticos q. circularon entonces
entre nosotros, nos prometiamos entrar en una era de felicidad, y esta
palabra, y lade libertad, heran las que tenian mas uso y mayor eco en
aquellos tiempos. Todo entonces se nos pintaba con color de rosa. Al
año de proclamada la Yndependencia dela Nacion, vimos por la
primera véz llegar á este Paiz comerciantes dela Republica vecina, q.
nos surtieron de generos mejores q. los que haviamos conocido hasta
entonces, y q. nos los vendian á unos precios sin comparacion mas
baratos q. aquellos enq. aconstumbrabamos comprarlos de inferior

calidad. Desde entonces siempre nos vinieron cada año mayores y mas variados surtidos de generos, y el espiritu de empresa mercantil se difundió tambien entre nosotros.

Se formaron desde luego compañias para hacer casar el castor en los rios de este Departamento; mas como el Gobⁿᵒ. Gгᾱl. tenia prohivida esta industria álos Estrangeros el Sʳ Gefe Politico del Departam.ᵗᵒ D. Bartolome Baca conla mira de familiarisar este arte entre nosotros, tomó sobre su responsabilidad el dar permisos para casar el castor álos partidos q. se despachaban si se componian de igual numero de nativos y de Estrangeros. Estos partidos de casadores no solo pescaban castor pero tambien trataban con los gentiles q. se manifestaban amigables. Para estos dos obgetos de casa y de trato en los paices de los Yndios, fué tal la empresa y el capital empleado que de solo el punto de Abiquiú salieron para los Estados Unidos del Norte 160. quintales de castor en un año q. al valor q. tenia en aquella epoca no importaba menos de alderredor de cien mil pesos duros. Las diferentes compañías q. se establecieron enla misma epoca en Taos, se supone que conciguieron proporcionalm.ᵗᵉ los mismos retornos pues se sabe que gastaban en abios y principalm.ᵗᵉ en caballada y bastimento de 50 á 60 mil pesos cada año.

En fin todo manifestaba mejora y prosperidad enlos primeros años dela Yndepend.ᵃ, pero no fue por desgracia de mucha duracion. El genio del mal pronto se ocupo en malear un bienestar tan venturoso para el Paiz. Algunos Señores á caso de buena fé pero imbuidos delas Dotrinas [sic] de otros siglos, y de otra clase de Gobⁿᵒ. trabajavan con empeño para restablecer el sistema *prohivitivo y de esclucion*; otros q. veian con embidia el provecho q. suponian les devian rendir el trafico y movimiento q. los Estrangeros daban á sus diferentes negocios (enlos q. tenian empleados á muchos Mejicanos[)], los denunciaban álas autoridades secreta ó publicam.ᵗᵉ como quebrantadores delas Leyes, y usurpadores de los veneficios q. esclucivam.ᵗᵉ correspondian á los Mejicanos, y afuerza de perseverar en este dañado principio lograron que las autoridades intimidadas por la responsabilidad con q. heran continuam.ᵗᵉ amenasadas les dieran oidos. Por estas causas á poco tiempo de relebado dela Gobernacion D. Bartolomé Baca, los empresarios Estrangeros, se bieron embueltos en pleitos y dificultades en tal grado q. al fin cansados de las persecuciones y cabilocidades de sus contrarios, y temiendo ademas porla seguridad de los resortes de sus especulaciones enlo futuro en este paiz, se fueron los mas al otro lado de nuestra frontera y establecieron ayi mas casas para el trato con los gentiles de aquellos parages porlos cuales paulatinamente fueron en cierto modo, escluidos los Nuevo Mejicos de ese comercio por no poder yá competir con aquellos establecimientos enlos precios delos generos porq. no pagan dr͞os. [derechos] de ellos á nadie.

Antes q. susediera esto, todas las espediciones de trato con aquellos gentiles salian de las poblaciones de este Departam.^to, y era inmensa la cantidad de cueros de cibulo [cíbolo] gamusas etc. que entraban al Pais, y q. despues se llebavan á tierra fuera.

Ahora apenas se ven cueros de cibulo, y se há disminuido tambien muchicimo el de las gamusas etc. quedando asi porla ignorancia, ó la maldad de unos cuantos, privado el Nuevo Mejico de ese comercio que le daba provecho é influencia con los gentiles, y q. al mismo tiempo aumentaba sus relaciones en el interior dela Republica. De ahi comensó esa decadencia q. tan aceleradamente nos bolvio á un grado de importancia y de riquesa muy inferior al q. teniamos por ese lado antes dela Yndependencia.

En la misma epoca, que por los medios q. se acaban de indicar se arruinaba al Nuevo Mejico en su comercio é importancia con los gentiles, se empesó á manifestar entre nosotros ese espiritu de aspirantismo ó empleomania deque desgraciadam.^te no estamos aun enteramente libres en nuestras transaciones politicas. Alucinados de estas miras mesquinas pocos se ocuparon delos verdaderos intereces del Paiz; el caso era de quien gosaria un destino por el cual pudiera vivir descansadamente á costa dela Nacion, sin nunca ser cuestion la capacidad delos individuos para desempeñarlos.

Los gentiles de alderredor de Nuevo Majico mejoraron en cierto modo de suerte, al mismo tiempo que se nos empeoraba la nuestra. El interes indujo muchos Americanos á establecer fuertes enlos Rios Chato, Arcansas, y Colorado, porlos cuales han sido ampliam.^te surtidos de cuanto nesecitan en cambio de sus peleterias. Por eso poco á poco nos fueron desconociendo y perdiendo el afecto todos los gentiles; y luego que se familiarisaron con las armas de fuego, y se vieron bien provistos de ellas no temieron yá ofendernos. Desde entonces tambien se notó q. progrecivamente el ganado cibulo q. otras veces hera tan abundante hasta en los egidos de nuestros poblados há ido desminuyendo tan aprisa q. yá se hase sentir su escaces, ó su falta absoluta en muchas partes, pues yá nuestros casadores ban ábuscarlo mas aya de cien leguas, y despues de un viaje dilatado de cuatro meses, hase dos años q. no hayan suficiente para acabarse de carne con que mantenerse para su buelta, sin trahér á sus casas ninguna; y en estas circunstancias los barvaros aguijoneados dela nesecidad, nos ostilisan para remediarse.

La generalidad delos Nuevo Mejicos, no há empeorado de la condicion en que se hallaban en tiempo del Gobierno Español; al contrario todo hombre de buena fé, confesará q. la han mejorado en muchos respectos pero los medios q. en aquellos tiempos los constituian ricos é invulnerables en sus hogares é imbencibles enlos campos de batalla, los constituyen ahora pobres y sin defensa.

Señores: los mas delos havitantes del Nuevo Mejico ó particularmente los q. estan mas espuestos álos ataques delos gentiles estan armados con solo arcos y flechas, y estas escasas porq. no tienen con que comprar mas, y mucho menos fuciles y municiones. El Supremo Gobño. dela Nacion continuamente distraido y ocupado de intereces mas generales, no há podido dispensarnos la proteccion q.^{e} nesecitamos y hubieramos deseado para nuestra seguridad. La poca tropa que hay en el Departam.^{to} está empleada en esta capital (que és el teatro delos partidos cuando los hay) en sostener las autoridades, y en conserbar el orden entre los havitantes; bien que aunq. estubiera libre de este servicio, por su numero, y por el estado de destitucion delos mas de los nesesarios, en q. se haya, no pudiera defender sino el punto donde se hallara, y nuestras dilatadas fronteras nesecitarian para ser defendidas militarmente segun el espiritu de arrogoencia [arrogancia] de nuestros varbaros enemigos, de miles de tropa disciplinada y asistida segun el sistema delos Precidiales aqui, en tiempo del Gobierno Español, cosa que el Erario Nacional no puede soportar.

De todos modos, esperar semejante proteccion del Supremo Gobño. dela Nacion, seria esperar en vano, particularm.^{te} en el estado há que está reducida la Republica por las diferentes facciones q. continuam.^{te} estan formando, los tambien diferentes intereces y el aspirantismo, porlo q. concidero q. para nuestra seguridad personal y la de nuestros intereces (en relacion álo menos á barvaros) no debemos contar con mas proteccion, ni recursos quelos de los propios Nuevo Mejicos; pero para q. estos puedan desplegar alguna nueva energia, debemos procurarles los medios de defensa, que son armas y municiones. Por una fatalidad siempre han faltado aqui estos dos renglones importanticimos, porq. aunque algunos ricos han adquirido de los comerciantes algunas de las armas de lujo que aquellos introdusen como para su uso, estas no están al alcanse dela generalidad, ni son tampoco comunm.^{te} los ricos los que salen á perceguir los varvaros cuando hán cometido

depredaciones. La introducion de armas y de municiones estan pro-
hividas por nuestras leyes, y el Gobierno no tiene aqui Depocito para el
Publico, del uno ni del otro renglon; y sin embargo nos son indispensables si queremos subsistir en este Departamento, y eso espuestos álos
mismo ó mayores horrores que los q. suseden en otros Departamentos
de mas poblacion y recursos q. el nuestro; en los cuales sin duda por
alguna delas mismas causas q. sufrimos aqui, no aciertan á bien
defenderse.

Señores: Las relaciones q. hé oido álos que tratan con las tribus varbaras, del numero de cautivos Mejicanos y particularm.te de Mugeres
jovenes tambien Mejicanas q. sirben álos vestiales plaseres delos gan-
dules barvaros, del trato brutal q. reciven, y de las clases de muerte q.
les suelen dar por cualesquier capricho me han hecho estremeser, me
han afligido, y me hán avergonsado al conciderar hasta donde percigue
la desventura á nuestra Nacion, y mas cuando contemplo cual sera á
caso la suerte de muchas personas q. aprecio, si con tiempo no se toman
medidas para precaver tan degradantes desgracias.

No dudo Señores; q. si el Pueblo de Nuevo Mejico, pudiera adquirir á
precios comodos armas y municiones, q. muy pronto los mismo barvaros q. ahora insultan nuestra inerme cituacion, aprenderian á su pro-
pia costa á respectarnos, ó mejor dicho, á temernos. Los indigenas gentiles no se han mejorado, ni en lo ficico, ni en lo moral, solo nuestra accidental debilidad constituye su fuerza.

Deseles álos Nuevo Mejicos, la facilidad de adquirir armas, é in-
spireceles por el amor patrio, por su interes, por su honor, y por la
varatura de estas, la inclinacion de ponerlas [en uso], y confío Señores,
q. si no decisten los barvaros de su presente conducta hacia nosotros, lo
repito, encontraron á pesar suyo con el castigo suficiente q. les
infligiran los desendientes de los antiguos descubridores y con-
quistadores de este inmenso continenti [sic].

La calidad y baratura delas armas y municiones, se conciguen por los
mismos medios q. la de cualesquiera otro renglon de comercio, porla
libre competicion entre los que las venden.

La rasa Española Señores, no há degenerado en Nuevo Mejico, como
bien lo atestiguan algunos hechos recientes aunque [?] parciales. La
suma de nuestras desgracias hasen yá anciar á todos los verdaderos hijos
del Paiz, por medios y ocaciones de coadyubar á nuestra seguridad, y
de provar a la Nacion, y al mundo entero que somos dignos por
nuestras virtudes de heredar en todo á nuestros ilustres antepasados.

El E.S. Gob.ʳ y comand.ᵗᵉ Gͬal. del Departam.ᵗᵒ D. Manuel Armijo q. afortunadam.ᵗᵉ há buelto á dirigir nuestros Destinos, no perdonará confio, medio ni fatigas para afiansarnos nuestra seguridad y bienestar, como no lo aseguran los susesos venturosos q. en tiempos anteriores, y con recursos arto [harto] escasos nos há conceguido por su actividad circunspeccion esperiencia y fortuna.

Para obtener tan apetecibles y felices obgetos propongo á esta honorable Asamblea, el que dirija al Soberano Congreso dela Nacion, una iniciativa fundada en las rasones q. acabo de esponer, y las demas q. S.E. estime condusentes, solicitando q. para remediar en lo pocible los males q. nos causan los barvaros, y para solo mientras duran estas nuestras criticas circunstancias q. se digne Decretar que.

Se permite la introducion de Armas y de municiones al Departam.ᵗᵒ de Nuevo Mejico libres de todo dͬro. [derecho].

Propongo tambien con el mismo obgeto el q. la Honorable Asamblea le embie á nuestro digno representante en el Congreso de la Union D. Tomas Chavez y Castillo, una copia dela anterior iniciativa con recomendacion particular para q. la apoyé, y active su pronto despacho, para q. si se obtiene un resultado favorable como és de esperarse, tenga noticia de ello en tiempo el comercio, y nos puedan venir este otoño ó temprano la primavera procsima los medios de asegurar nuestra existencia y propiedades. Santa Fe Junio 18. de 1846.

Donaciano Vigil [signature]

III

Vigil on the Maladministratión of New Mexico under Governors Pérez and Martínez and under Commanding General García Conde[1]

June 22, 1846

Honorable Assembly

The nation is about to restructure itself once again.[2] Therefore, I believe it would be an opportune and very useful occasion for this Assembly to commission New Mexico's representative to request from the proper authorities that in the future the political and military commands of this Department be entrusted to people who are either natives of it, or who have resided among us long enough before their nomination to know our interests and the various needs that arise from our peculiar situation.

This proposition, whose purpose is to assure the peace and security of New Mexico, might perhaps be attributed to a spirit of localism by those who know neither our situation nor our history. But this Assembly, and those observant men who have noticed the vicissitudes that some administrations have caused us by not having met these requirements, will surely exempt me from such petty motives.

The peculiar location of our country, surrounded on all sides by heathen Indians who harass us most of the time; the extreme poverty in which these circumstances keep the majority of our fellow citizens (for which reason it has not been possible, nor will it be possible, to establish a direct tax for a long time); and the scarcity and irregularity of revenue which is needed to meet the most urgent needs, reduces New Mexico to a state of anxiety and distress. I am pleased to believe that this is not experienced to the same degree in any other department of the Republic.

Due to our situation, then, our needs are great. Thus it is no wonder that when the central government sends us officials to fill either the political or military command, or the two together, they find themselves perplexed. These officials, whose talents and services rendered in other places have won the government's trust, are accustomed to the customs and management of the departments of the interior, whose population, enlightenment, and wealth only require making good use of resources. Arriving in New Mexico, where those elements are lacking, these officials have not figured out how to use or manage our resources, such as they are, either for peace or for war. Not having sufficiently considered our circumstances, and wanting to conform their government to what laws and circumstances require or allow in the rest of the departments of the Republic, some have left us bad memories of their administration.

I shall explain this better by relating some summarized fragments of our history of the last ten years.

Sr. Alvino Pérez came to New Mexico in 1835 with the best recommendations of the central government, of the ministerial newspapers, and of many other newspapers of the interior.[3] As soon as this gentleman arrived in Santa Fe, he surrounded himself with the most learned men of the country who were also, in his opinion, the purest patriots. He delivered himself entirely to their counsels. With the help of these men he did not hesitate, as he himself expressed on several occasions, to establish the government of New Mexico on a footing analogous to the constitution and current laws of the Republic.[4] He cut out by the roots the abuses of the old colonial system and the other irregularities that he observed and attributed to the ignorance or lack of zeal of former governors. The people of New Mexico did not doubt the good intentions of Sr. Pérez. Even now, in spite of the events that he brought on the country (his conduct now belongs to history), most are persuaded that if the happiness of New Mexico could possibly have depended on the good intentions and the concern of this man, he would have secured it for us. But in spite of such good intentions, his lack of practical knowledge of the character, interests, and traditional customs of New Mexicans caused him to make mistakes that brought us days so bitter that their only parallel in our history is the general revolt of the Indians in the year 1664.[5]

In his choice of political appointments, he completely neglected the consideration due to the class that is influential because of its wealth. Although these people were not endowed with the knowledge that Sr. Pérez believed indispensable to perform their duties, the fact was that these people, feeling snubbed, naturally tried to discredit Sr. Pérez. The favored employees, certain of the implicit confidence Sr. Pérez placed in them from the beginning, took advantage of it more than should have been tolerated. By this means, they also helped the declared enemies of Sr. Pérez to discredit his administration.

In the campaign that Sr. Pérez launched against the Navajos, he won very important advantages. When, as a result of that, however, he sought a peace treaty with them, he also showed he knew neither the temperment of the savages nor any of the cleverness they employ. He was a toy of the Navajo negotiators. They diverted him with beautiful promises and distracted him with lengthy discussions about the time and place of the next meeting until they gained with no difficulty the objectives they sought. This resulted in very great financial losses for our fellow citizens. Since they were under arms, and for much more time than necessary, they had abandoned all their own interests.[6] With this, Sr. Pérez gave his enemies an opportunity to discredit him. They took advantage of it by circulating among the people and speaking enthusiastically of his mistakes, exaggerating all of their circumstances.

In obedience to repeated orders from his superiors, Sr. Pérez tried to take the first steps to establish direct taxation in this Department (something which these inhabitants have always resisted, based on terms granted to the settlers, who are always subject to many hardships, expenses, and risks which they take freely). All the permanent troops had been put on leave for some time, due to lack of resources. Even though at this same time the caravan from the United States arrived, either because it produced little [revenue], or because of embezzlement, or maybe both things, the fact was that the solemn contracts agreed to by the government were not satisfied.[7] The troops remained disbanded. The conduct of the favorites of Sr. Pérez made him more unpopular each day through their indiscretions, their lack of good faith in [payment of] contracts, and the contempt which they held for public opinion and the complaints of the offended.

This combination of circumstances now displeased not only those who were truly victims of the administration, but also those who had public spirit, those who felt passed over for government jobs, and the people in general who could see that the fortunes of New Mexico, far from improving, were moving at a more rapid pace toward total ruin.

Sr. Pérez's enemies diligently took advantage of these circumstances to alarm the people by exaggerating how unjust and exorbitant the taxes were that officials tried to impose on them. Sr. Pérez's enemies persuaded the people by making use of the pretext given to them by some of the excessive and illegal conduct of his favorites. Sr. Pérez's enemies said that these taxes emanated from the government of Santa Fe alone, to be used for financing the disorders and extravagances of its employees. As soon as the people were driven to a certain degree of discontent, distrust, and agitation by the aforementioned means, the tenacious enemies of Sr. Pérez planned a rebellion. Its ostensible purpose was only to remove the favorites of Sr. Pérez from their positions. Toward this end, they formed *juntas* of the upper class at various places in Río Arriba. At first, these did no more than request that Sr. Pérez dismiss those employees.[8]

Sr. Pérez knew perfectly well the perpetrators of all these movements and their goal, which was his destruction and that of all his employees. However, having contempt for their leaders and the means they employed, he persisted in following the advice of his favorites despite the opinion of circumspect and well-intentioned people who longed only for the tranquility of the country. He did not apprehend the leaders of the revolution, nor place the troops under arms. Instead, with just two hundred conscripted men under the immediate command of persons under the influence of his opponents, he proceeded to his encounter on August 7, 1837. He believed that with these troops he would command the respect of the rebellious crowd. The final result was that [*] Sr. Pérez, his secretary, the district judge, the prefect of the 1st district, and various other civilian and military officials and other citizens in his service, were murdered by their cruel enemies — not to mention those who died in the battle.[9]

So it was that with the best intentions and better than average quali-

---

*At this place, the copy of this document in the Mexican Archives of New Mexico (roll 41, frame 343) includes the following words, which are crossed out: "on the twelfth of the same month the priest Martínez sang the Te Deum Laudamus in the church of the Lord of Esquipulas of Chimayó [several words illegible] because. . . ."

fications of talent and courage, a governor and military commander from the interior caused a bloody revolution in which he himself perished, and which endangered even the integrity of the Republic, because he lacked knowledge of the character of these inhabitants — their needs, their opinions, and their traditional concerns. I believe it is useful that these facts be put on the record just as they happened, in order to serve the government in the future and so they will not be distorted by the credence that could be given to what the true perpetrators of the revolution, among others, have had said to D.C.M.B. [don Carlos María Bustamante], in his *memorias* on the history of Mexico.[10]

Sr. don Manuel Armijo, present Governor and Comandante General of this Department, at the head of those who love order and constitutional government, was the one who had the honor of drowning the revolutionary hydra in 1837 and reestablishing order and peace among us. This is the place to recount the main events of his administration, in order to compare it with that of Sr. Pérez, which I have just described, and with the one that followed it of Sr. don Mariano Martínez. With only the same resources that the latter two gentlemen had had, Sr. Armijo was fortunate enough to keep peace in New Mexico, and to make it more respected abroad than in any other period since Independence. Since this man directs the destinies of the country at the present time, however, it would appear to be flattery on my part to recount his services. I will limit myself to say that by employing either moral or physical force alternatively, depending upon the circumstances, he subdued revolutionaries on two successive occasions: he defeated the Texan expedition that came to invade us; and he made the heathen who surround New Mexico respect it, much more than in the two periods to which I have just referred — perhaps, also, more than at any other time since Independence.[11]

Sr. General don Mariano Martínez came to us from outside on December 8, 1843, as Commandante General of the Department, and on the 15th of the following May he received the governorship of the Department because this Assembly, to his good fortune, recommended him.[12]

The beginning of this man's administration was not noteworthy due to any important event. One notes only the indiscretion with which he made unfavorable comparisons of the culture of the inhabitants of this Department with those of others; his great resolve to reform, improve, and regenerate, believing everything that had already been established here as defective and absurd; and the pleasure with which he received the flattery that his secretaries and other gentlemen of his retinue bestowed upon him all the time.[13]

All of this certainly had nothing more wrong with it, nor any other consequence, than to allow the public to observe his feeble mind. It seemed that the chief function of his devotees was to eulogize him and to enumerate the great things which he proposed to do in the future to assure the happiness of the Department — all of which, nevertheless, was always left for the future.

Later on, since the Navajos stole herds of cattle with impunity on the frontiers, some residents of Taos requested and received permission from the previous government to make war on them. In a short campaign, those volunteers were fortunate enough to punish the Navajos, killing their men, seizing a herd of horses, and bringing back a few captives. But, since at that time there were Utes among the Navajos, the Utes also suffered part of the punishment intended for the Navajos. Not long after this, the Utes demanded the freedom of the prisoners taken from their tribe, as well as payment for those who had been killed mistakenly. The Justice of the Peace of Abiquiú and the Ute's interpreter informed Sr. Martínez of their claims. In response, he issued orders and terms of such a nature that they neither satisfied the Utes, nor could be carried out by the judge of that frontier region. Ignorant of the circumstances of a justice of the peace of a poor border settlement, Sr. Martínez gave him orders that at times the commander-in-chief of a victorious army might imprudently impose on a conquered foe. Thus the poor frontier judge, wanting to obey orders from above as much as possible, notified the Utes and achieved nothing more than winning their contempt. The Utes consequently committed many excesses in the jurisdiction of Abiquiú and mocked the orders of Sr. Governor Martínez.

At once the Utes went to Río Arriba, where the prefect of that district lived, to make the same request of him for satisfaction, but he was equally lacking in the means or the authority to satisfy them. Unable to restrain them, he referred them to the governor himself in Santa Fe, hoping this gentleman would have enough good judgment and strength of character to remedy that which he found so bad and that which his powerless subordinates could not accomplish despite repeated orders.

One hundred and some Utes arrived at Santa Fe. Depositing their equipment and arms, as was their custom, and placing their horse herd under the care of the troops, nine *capitancillos*[14] went to see Sr.

Martínez. The rest of the Indians scattered around the city in stores and houses, trying to trade for what they needed. During their visit to Sr. Martínez, the *capitancillos* stated their complaints and, after accomplishing this in some way, went on to explain that it was an established custom for them to receive gifts every time they visited the governor of New Mexico, whether for some reason or simply because they wanted to. When they saw the gifts, the *capitancillos* noticed a great decrease in what they were accustomed to receive. They told Sr. Martínez, naturally using words which expressed their feelings toward him. They declared that although they had been offended, the governor wanted to give them less than when they had been friends without complaints, when they received presents as a mere reward and expression of their alliance. Sr. Martínez replied somewhat in the spirit in which he had given the orders to the frontier justice of the peace. One of the *capitancillos*, wanting to tell Sr. Martínez how unjust he was, and wishing to make use of all eloquence, which among the Indians consists of words as well as motions and gestures, told him among other things: "Since you come from another land that is so poor that it needed what the government gave to its Indian allies, you have come a great distance to put Utes and New Mexicans on bad terms, although they have lived in solid peace and understanding for many generations."

Either intimidated or shamed by this sharp reproach, which is so natural for the Indians, Sr. Martínez cried out so that the guards heard and responded. In spite of the fact that the *capitancillos* were unarmed and could have been arrested and punished, they were all barbarously murdered by his order along with some other Indians who were in the immediate vicinity. During the tumult caused by the slaughter, the rest of the Indians either noticed or learned what was happening and ran toward the place where they had left their equipment and arms. Fearing what could happen to them, they withdrew hurriedly down the main street in a group. They feared they would be pursued, but the few soldiers who followed them always maintained a good distance, for after the Indians joined together the soldiers killed only two Indians.

At the same time that the Indians were coming down the main street, their herd of 105 horses, driven by the soldiers, entered the *Plaza* through [John] Scolly's alley and were placed in the corral of the *Palacio*. Many people thought then that since Sr. Martínez had started the hostilities, he would take advantage of the saddles and horses of the Utes, and arrange for the troops to trail them until finishing them off. But Sr. Martínez did not deem it desirable, even though he was advised that the *ranchería* of these Utes was in Abiquiú, and it would be easy to go and seize their families before the fugitives got there and thus reestablish peace with them. If the Utes were given time, however, they would avenge the losses they had incurred by catching the poor residents of the frontier unprepared. Sr. General Martínez did not believe it necessary to expend so much energy against a contemptible enemy, nor did he consider it desirable to halt the great preparations he was making for a bull fight. So he neither went himself nor sent anyone against the Utes.[15]

Notwithstanding the firm stand this gentleman had taken, he struggled to calm some of the residents who expressed some apprehension for the jurisdiction of Río Arriba. He assured them that the Utes would flee far away without resting. Afterwards, even if they united in great numbers, they were not capable of taking the offensive and even less capable of taking Santa Fe, etc. He erred completely on the first point and spoke nonsense in regard to the second. Besides being one of the few focal points of the department, Santa Fe has all the troops of the country for its garrison. While Sr. Martínez devoted himself entirely to his bulls, to the security of Santa Fe, and to his esteemed person, the Utes were slaughtering almost at will the most respectable citizens of Abiquiú. Among the victims who perished in the area of Abiquiú as a result of Sr. Martínez's blameworthy stupidity, allow me gentlemen to make special mention of captains Vigil and Salazar, because both had rendered important services to the nation, and because both died as brave men following severe stabbings in their chests.

Not even when the news of the deaths perpetrated by the Utes in Abiquiú reached Santa Fe, did Sr. Martínez take any steps to protect the frontiers. He directed all of his efforts toward his own personal security and that of his command, which his followers had led him to believe was in danger. They assured him that the language the Utes used with him, as well as their recent outrages on the frontiers, represented the handiwork of his enemies who employed them for the purpose of distracting him and surprising him if he sent out the troops. Nevertheless, due to the strength of the protests made to him, he made an effort to pull himself together and sent a small detachment to the towns of Abiquiú, Rito, and Ojo Caliente.

General Martínez distingushed himself not only for his great ignorance of our situation and our relations with neighboring heathen tribes, but also demonstrated either ignorance or willful neglect of the most basic principles of the art of warfare. Among other things, one should annihilate the enemy or gain the best possible advantage from him. Sr. Martínez had a very decided advantage. But no, because of his fatal ignorance of our situation or because of his false pride at the thoughtless words of a wretched barbarian, he ushered us into a bloody war with a courageous and combat-hardened tribe with whom we had been on friendly terms since time immemorial.[16] We had been so close that on many occasions the Utes, as our allies, generously shed their blood at our side, fighting against the enemies of New Mexico. Sr. Martínez's concern about the danger of a revolution against his administration, in which the Utes might take part, was so great that when anyone suggested how advantageous it would be to send a force against the Utes, it was always his weakness to try to persuade that person that the danger point was Santa Fe. Regarding the Utes, he would punish them severely in the spring, carrying the war to their homes. He expounded on his campaign plans and the tactics he intended to use to defeat the Utes. He did not consider that if all of his great imaginary movements should take place in the land of the Utes, they would be in mountains so rugged that there are no trails other than those made by wild sheep and rabbits. Finally, the more effort he made to justify his inaction and his hopes, the more he made a fool of himself. All of New Mexico knows through experience that in wars against the heathens (excepting secret marches and combined attacks), the battle always depends upon the personal efforts of individuals, with no other rule or tactic than each one's particular fighting skill.

At the same time that Sr. Martínez severely endangered the security of the Department by making external enemies, he promoted discontent among his own people. If his administration had lasted a bit longer it might have faced some [internal] disorder. Thus, either through weakness or with the full intent of satisfying the needs of his favorites, he authorized the practice of certain arbitrary acts. The means were so illegal that only the meekness and lack of resources of those who suffered most from them permitted these things to occur so quietly. I shall relate some of the most important. First, a resident of Taos who had premeditatedly killed another, dragging him by an arm from a saddle horn, fled the country to avoid the punishment that awaited him. He returned in 1844 and upon arrival was imprisoned in the jail of this city. He was set free without anyone knowing the means the government used to justify it. The fact is that he undoubtedly used such persuasive language with Sr. Martínez and with his advisors, that without any kind of judgment or acquittal from any competent tribunal, the criminal was absolved. He returned to his home where he has lived since then, enjoying as much peace as any other honest and innocent man, in spite of his guilty conscience. Second, an American had been murdered on the frontier of this department and his killers had been discovered and justly pursued at the urging of the American consul. The murdered man's properties had been placed at the disposal of the consul, and considerable correspondence concerning this matter took place with the government. At the request of his favorites, Sr. Martínez permitted the murdered man's property to be *ostensibly* invested in public funds or in his pocket. Thus, for his own profit, Martínez made this Department and the Republic vulnerable to charges of a shocking injustice which the United States might make some day.[17]

General Martínez had the good fortune that the various caravans which arrived from the United States yielded more [revenue] during his administration than they had during previous years. Besides this, during his term a tax was established on goods proceeding from the interior of the Republic. This gentleman made so much use of the credit these circumstances gave him that he borrowed considerable sums from the capitalists of the Río Abajo. Notwithstanding all of these advantages, which his predecessors lacked, payment to the army was irregular. The troops manifested their discontent on several occasions and their discipline and obedience declined noticeably. While the troops suffered great privations and received most of their pay in merchandise which was not useful to them, or whose use was prohibited by ordinance, as are playing cards and brandy, some of Martínez's favorites received their wages months in advance. Because of this kind of management, Sr. Martínez established an unenviable reputation among responsible people. As a result of this management, the national treasuries were emptied and credit ran out. Later, then, he was in such dire straits that in spite of the general poverty of the country, we have seen few times like those.[18]

It was then that he strongly demanded the influence that his position in the Department gave him, and especially with most of the members of this Honorable Assembly. By using the pretext of invasions of Texans and Indians, he caused this same Honorable Assembly to order a forced loan, contrary to law, custom, and propriety, which was carried out in the most absurd and arbitrary manner possible. The contributing class was not represented. The allotments were assigned capriciously, not on the basis of one's capital assets and with no guidelines at all. One resident, who was declared a foreigner a few days before this decree was issued, was assessed 600 pesos. For defending his rights he was put in the public jail.[19] People in charge of the stores in Santa Fe, which belonged to some gentlemen from Río Abajo who had been assessed for the compulsory loan and who refused to make the payment in their home towns, were also put in jail. They were finally obliged to let Sr. Martínez's agent collect in the stores the payment owed by the absent store owners. In the jurisdiction of Taos, two of the people required to pay the loan (one ill in bed and the other absent) came under suspicion for failing to pay. They were persecuted as if they were worse than criminals who had done harm to the nation. The son of one of them was required to come from San Fernando de Taos to Río Arriba so that he might answer and pay for his father. Because of these arbitrary and gouging tendencies, Sr. Martínez won the enmity of all the native and foreign merchants. Also, it is the fault of Martínez that the resident who declared himself a foreigner, along with another from the same nation and class, will make declarations concerning the injustices they have suffered to the minister of his British Majesty (of whom, both were born subjects). The Mexican government may have [already?] taken both cases under consideration.[20]

After causing these injuries to New Mexico, Sr. Martínez left at the order of the central government to enjoy the pleasures of private life. It is asserted that he still owed large sums to different individuals in this Department, including a debt of 18,000 pesos to don Antonio Sandoval. I do not doubt that this, along with his administrative measures, perpetuates his memory, but not to his advantage.[21]

Sr. General Martínez was succeeded in the military command by Sr. don Francisco García Conde, as Commanding General of the Fifth Division.[22] This man did not stay among us long enough to enable us to appreciate adequately all of his good qualities which we must suppose abound in his character. Notwithstanding the brevity of his visit, we could not help but notice that, due to some error perhaps, he took measures in New Mexico that did not give a favorable opinion of his principles. He had hardly arrived when he put himself in competition with the political authorities and the treasury employees because he wanted to assume powers that were not his. In spite of the high esteem which nearly everyone in New Mexico held for him because of his high rank, they believed that the offended parties were correct in resisting him. One of his measures in regard to the military, which discredited him entirely with this class of worthy citizens, was to promote an honest but ignorant rancher from a militia officer to the Comandante General of New Mexico over a large number of veteran officers, one of them of high rank.[23] In spite of the resistance he encountered from the political and treasury authorities, Sr. García Conde found a way to take possession of a large sum of money that was in the national treasuries. This was earmarked, in part, to pay the compulsory government loan. Sr. García Conde took this money from the hands of the treasurer by force, and in order to accomplish his purpose he imprisoned this employee.[24] The compulsory government loan was backed by the public faith, and the solemn promise of the government and of the Honorable Assembly. Efforts were made in vain to show him how shameful it was to break faith in similar contracts. This gentleman insisted upon going ahead with his plan with the pretext of wanting to buy saddles and horses for the presidial soldiers of New Mexico. With the pretext, also, of conveying these two items, he took with him two officials who, as members of the Honorable Assembly, had in some manner opposed his plans. All of you gentlemen know that the two officials have returned to Santa Fe and that they have brought neither the saddles nor the herd of horses.[25] Now there are not even hopes that they will ever arrive. Before leaving us, Sr. García Conde was good enough to favor New Mexico by relieving the treasury officials of their jobs, although those officials had merited the confidence of the central government which had assigned them to the aforementioned and qualified military commander.[26]

It is on these facts, gentlemen, that I base my opinion, wishing that the political and military commands of New Mexico might be given to natives or residents of the Department, so they might be involved in our interests and our aspirations. Even assuming that those who are named for these positions are not gifted with great talents, we may at least be spared of the vicissitudes that señores Pérez, Martínez, and García Conde have caused us.

Thus I conclude, proposing to the Honorable Assembly that it send instructions to our worthy representative in the National Congress, don Tomás Chávez y Castiyo, to ask the proper authority that the political and military commands of this Department always be given to people who have lived long enough among us to know our situation and our true interests intimately.

> Santa Fe, June 22, 1846
> Donaciano Vigil [signature]

IV

Vigil opina sobre la maladministración de Nuevo México bajo los Gobernadores Pérez y Martínez, y bajo el Comandante General García Conde

22 Junio 1846

Honorable Asamblea

Estando para constituirse de nuevo la Nacion, creo la ocacion oportuna y muy util al Nuevo Mejico, que V.E. encargue á nuestro representante, que solicite dela autoridad á quien corresponda que enlo futuro los mandos Politico y Militar de este Departam.^{to} sean confiados á personas nativas de el ó que hayan recidido entre nosotros el tiempo suficiente anteriormente á su nominacion para conoser nuestros intereces y las diferentes nesecidades que nos causa lo peculiar de nuestra cituacion.

Esta propocicion cuyo obgeto es asegurar la tranquilidad y seguridad del pais, á caso se atribuirá á espiritu de localidad porlos que no conosen ni nuestra cituacion ni nuestra historia; pero V.E. y los hombres observadores que hán notado las vicicitudes que algunas administraciones nos han acarreado por falta de estos requicitos me libraran seguram.^{te} de miras tan mesquinas.

Lo peculiar de la localidad de nuestro Paiz cercado por todos rumbos de Yndios gentiles q. nos ostilizan lo mas del tiempo; la pobresa estremada en q. estas circunstancias mantienen ála generalidad de nuestros conciudadanos (por cuya causa no se há podido ni se podrá en mucho tiempo establecer una contribucion directa) y lo escaso y eventual delas rentas conq. se atienden cuando se puede álas nesecidades mas urgentes, reducen al Nuevo Mejico á una ecsistencia de apuros y anciedades q. me plasco en creer ningun otro Departamento de la Republica esperimenta en igual grado.

Por esto no és de estrañar deq. cuando el Supremo Gobierno nos há embiado para uno ú otro mando ó los dos juntos señores oficiales que por sus talentos y servicios en otras partes habian merecido su confianza; como aconstumbrados á los estilos y manejos delos Departamentos delo interior enlos q. su poblacion ilustracion y riqueza solo se nesecita de hacer buen uso de sus recursos, llegando á nuestro pais donde esos elementos faltan, y q.^{e} por razon de nuestra cituacion las nesecidades son muchas, se hallan visto perplejos, y no hayan asertado á usar ó á dar direccion álos recursos del Paiz tales como ellos son, ni para la páz, ni p^a la guerra; y que otros por no tomar suficientemente en concideracion nuestras circunstancias y queriendo asimilar su gobernacion álo que las Leyes y las circunstancias ecsijen ó permiten enlos demas Departamentos dela Republica, nos han dejado recuerdos poco gratos de su admon. [administración].

Esto lo esplicaré mejor relacionando algunos fragmentos compendiados en nuestra historia enlos ultimos dies años.

El Sr D. Alvino Perez vino al Nuevo Mejico en 1.835. anunciado con las majores recomendaciones del Supremo Gobno. de los periodicos ministeriales y de otros muchos periodicos del interior. Apenas llegó este S^r á Santa Fee se rodeó de los hombres mas instruidos del paiz, y al mismo tiempo á su entender de los mas puros patriotas, y se entregó enteramente á sus concejos. Con el aucilio de estos no dudó segun se espresó el mismo en varias ocaciones de establecer la gobernacion en Nuevo Mejico sobre un pie analogo ála constitucion y Leyes Vigentes de la Republica cortando de raiz los abusos del antiguo sistema colonial, y las otras irregularidades q. observaba y q. atribuia ála ignorancia ó falta de celo delos anteriores gobernadores. El Pueblo de Nuevo Mejico no dudaba delos buenos propositos del Sr Perez, y ahora mismo á pesar de los eventos que acarreó al Paiz, y que en conducta pertenese ála historia, la generalidad está persuadida de que si la felicidad de Nuevo Mejico hubiera podido depender de solo las buenas intenciones y desvelos de este Sor., que nos la hubiera procurado. Mas á pesar de tan buenas disposiciones la falta de conocimientos practicos del caracter, intereces y constumbres tradicionales de los Nuevo Mejicos le hicieron cometer errores que nos causaron dias tan amargos que solo tienen paralelo en nuestra historia, enlos dela sublevacion general delos Yndigenas el año de 1.664.

En la eleccion que hiso para los Empleos de su nominacion descuidó enteramente la concideracion que se debia á la clase influyente por su caudal, bien que no estaba adornada de los conocimientos q. á el le parecian indispensables para desempeñarlos, y el caso fué que estos conciderandose desairados trataron desde luego de desprestigiar al Sr Perez. Los Empleados favoritos seguros dela implicita confianza q. dicho S^r puso en ellos desde el principio abusaban de ella mas de lo que se debia tolerar, y por este medio tambien coadyubarón con los declarados enemigos del Sr Perez en desprestigiar su Gobierno. En la campaña que hiso el S̄or. Peréz á Nabajó consiguió ventajas bastante importantes, pero cuando de resultas de ella se trató de hacer las paces con ellos, tambien manifestó q. no conocia ni el genio de los salvajes ni ningunas delas mañas q. usan, pues fue juguete delos negociadores Nabajoés que lo divirtieron con bellas promesas y prolongaron la reunion ála citacion y avenimiento de lugar de ella hasta q. lograron sin ningun incombeniente los obgetos q. tenian ála mira con grandicimos perjuicios de nuestros conciudadanos q. tenian abandonados todos sus intereces por estar sobre las armas, y esto mucho mas del tiempo nesesario. Con esto el Sr Perez dió ocacion que aprovecharon sus enemigos circulando y ponderando estas faltas entre el Pueblo para desconceptuarlo ecsajerando todas las circunstancias de ellas.

Cuando en obediensia de repetidas ordenes superiores trató el Sr Perez de dar los primeros pasos para establecer en este Departamento la contribucion directa (cosa que estos havitantes siempre han recistido fundados á demas en los terminos concedidos á los pobladores, á que estan siempre sugetos á muchas fatigas costos y riesgos q. rinden gratuitamente) estaba toda la tropa permanente hacia yá tiempo dada de baja por falta de recursos: y aunque por este mismo tiempo llegó la carabana delos Estados Unidos sea porq. esta rindió poco ó porq. hubo mala versacion ó acaso ambas cosas juntas el caso fue que los compromisos solemnes de contratos dela Gobernacion no fueron satisfechos; la tropa permanecio disuelta, y la conducta delos favoritos del Sr Perez lo hacian cada dia mas impopular por sus indiscrecciones, por su falta de fé en los contratos y por el desprecio con que concideraban la opinion Publica y las quejas delos agrabiados. El conjunto de estos hechos tenian yá disgustados á ademas delos que heran verdaderam.^{te} victimas de la Admōn. álos que tenian espiritu Publico, álos que se concideraban postergados enlos Destinos, y al Pueblo en

general que veia que lejos de mejorarse la suerte de Nuevo Mejico concideraban que corria aceleradam.^{te} á su total ruina. Los enemigos del
Sr Perez aprovecharon diligentem.^{te} estas circunstancias para alarmar
el Pueblo con ecsajeraciones delo injusto, y ecsorvitante de las contribuciones que intentaban imponerle, persuadiendole valiendose de
los pretestos q. les daban algunos de los ecsesos é ilegalidades dela conducta de sus favoritos, que las tales contribuciones emanaban de solo la
gobernacion de Santa Fé con el obgeto de atender con ellas álos
desordenes y estrabagancias delos mismos Empleados. Luego q. por los
medios indicados fue el Pueblo conducido á cierto grado de descontento, de desconfianza y de ecsaltacion, los tenaces enemigos del Sr Perez,
planaron una rebolucion q.^e tenia por obgeto ostencible de solo quitar
de sus Destinos álos actuales favoritos de dh̄o. S̄ōr. Con este fin se
hicieron juntas dela gente mas ecsaltada en varios puntos de arriba
enlas cuales al principio no se pretendia mas que solicitar esto mismo
del Sr Perez. Este S̄ōr. que conocia perfectam.^{te} los autores de todos
estos movimientos y el obgeto q. tenian ála mira q. hera la de su
destruccion y la de todos los Empleados pero q. despreciando los
motores, y los medios q. empleaban percistió en seguir los concejos de
sus favoritos á pesar dela opinion de gente circunspecta y bien inten-
cionada que solo anciaba por la tranquilidad del Paiz; no se aseguró
delos gefes dela rebolucion ni puso la tropa sobre las armas, sino q. con
solo unos doscientos hombres de leva al mando inmediato de personas
q. dependian de sus contrarios, creyendo que con ellos impondria
respecto ála multitud sublevada, marcho á su encuentro el 7 de Agosto
de 1.837. y el resultado final fue que [*] el mismo Sr Pérez su S̄rio. el
Juez de Distrito, el Prefecto del 1er Distrito y otros varios oficiales
civiles, y militares, y otros ciudadanos afectos á su servicio havian
asecinados por sus crueles enemigos independientemente delos q.^e
sucumbieron en el combate.

Asi fue como con las mejores intenciones y con calificaciones de
talento y valor mas de medianas un Gobernador y Comand.^{te} Militar
venido del interior por carecer de conocimiento del caracter de estos

---

*At this place, the copy of this document in the Mexican Archives of New Mexico (roll 41,
frame 343) includes the following words, which are crossed out: "el 12 del mismo fue can-
tado el *te deum laudamus* por el Sr. cura Martínez en el Santuario del Sr. de Esquipulas de
Chimayó [several words illegible] por que. . . ."

havitantes, de sus nesecidades, de sus opiniones, y de sus preocupaciones tradicionales, causo una rebolucion sangrienta enla cual el mismo pereció, y que puso en peligro hasta la integridad dela Republica. Estos hechos creo util que sean constantes tales como susedieron para que sirva de gobierno en lo futuro, y para q. no sean desfigurados por el credito que pudiera darse álo que los verdaderos autores dela rebolucion han hecho decir entre otros á D. C. M. B. en sus memorias para la historia de Mejico.

El Sr D. Manuel Armijo actual Gob.^r y Comand.^{te} G̅r̅al. de este Departamento fué el que ála cabesa de los amantes del orden y del gobierno constitucional tubo el honor de ahogar la hidra rebolucionaria en 1.837. y de restablecer entre nosotros el orden y la páz. Aqui correspondiera referir lo principal de su administracion para compararla con la que acabo de relacionar del Sr Perez y la que le susedio del Sr D. Mariano Martinez pues q. con solos los mismos recursos q. esos dos Señores habian tenido tubo la fortuna de mantener la paz en el Nuevo Mejico, y de hacerlo respetar en lo exterior mas q. en ningun otro tiempo desde la Yndependencia, pero como este S^r rige los Destinos del Paiz enla actualidad y que porlo mismo pareciera adulacion mia el relatar sus servicios, me limitaré á decir que usando alternativam.^{te} segun las circunstancias dela fuerza moral ó dela ficica sugetó en dos ocasiones subsecivas [sucesivas] los rebolucionarios rindió la espediccion Tejana que bino á imbadirnos, é hiso respetar el Nuevo Mejico porlos gentiles q. lo circundan, mucho mas enlo que lo fue enlas dos epocas que acabo de referir, y acaso tambien mas q. ninguna otra despues dela Yndependencia.

El S^r G̅r̅al. D. Mariano Martinez nos vino de afuera el 8 de Diciembre de 1843. de Comand.^{te} G̅r̅al. del Departam.^{to} y en 15 de Mayo siguiente se recivió del gob̅n̅o. del mismo por haverlo puesto V.E. misma en su quinterna en lugar preferente.

El principio de su adm̅o̅n. de este S̅o̅r. no fue notable por ningun evento de importancia, solo sele notó la indiscreccion con que hacia comparaciones poco favorables dela ilustracion de los havitantes de este Departam.^{to} con los de otros lo mucho que se proponia reformar, mejorar, y regenerar, en este Paiz conciderando todo lo establecido hasta aqui como vicioso y absurdo y la complaciencia conque el recivia el incienso que sus S̅r̅i̅o̅s̅. y demas S̅r̅e̅s̅. de su sequito le ofrecian á cada instante.

Todo esto por supuesto no tenia mas de malo, ni tenia otra concecuensia que el dejar percivir del Publico lo devil de su entendimiento pues que parecia q.^{e} el principal oficio de sus allegados hera el de hacer su panegirico y de representar en prespectiva [sic] las grandes cosas que se proponia hacer mas adelante para asegurar la felicidad del Departamento y que sin embargo dejo siempre todo en prespectiva.

Pero mas adelante como los Nabajoés cometian impunemente rovos de ganados enlas fronteras algunos vecinos de Taos pidieron y obtubieron dela gobernacion anterior permiso para hacerles la guerra. Una corta campaña voluntaria delos dhōs. vecinos tubo la suerte de castigar los Nabajoes matandoles hombres, quitandoles caballada y trayendose algunas piezas cautivas; pero como ála sason habia entre los Nabajoes Yndios Yutas estos tambien sufrieron su parte en el castigo q. se destinaba á aquellos. Los Yutas reclamaron poco despues la libertad delos pricioneros enla tribu, y el pago delas muertes q. equivocadamente se les habian hecho. El Juez de paz de Abiquiú y el Ynterprete delos Yutas informaron al Sr Martinez de sus pretenciones y sobre ello este S^r dió tales ordenes y dictó tales dispociciones ni fueron satisfechos los Yutas, ni el Juez de aquella frontera pudo egecutarlas. Ygnorante delas circunstancias de un Juez de paz de una pobre poblacion de frontera le dió ordenes q. á veces el Gefe de un Ejercito vencedor fuera imprudente de imponer á pueblo yá vencido: asi és que el pobre Juez dela frontera queriendo obedecer hasta donde pudo sus ordenes superiores selas notificó, y no conciguió mas q.^{e} atraherse el desprecio delos Yutas que cometieron por ello bastantes ecsesos enla jurisdicicion [sic] de Abiquiú y que rediculisaron las ordenes del Sr Gob.^{r} Martinez. En seguida los Yutas fueron al Rio Arriba donde recidia el Prefecto de aquel Distrito para pedirle la satisfaccion yá mencionada pero este S^r igualm.^{te} sin medios y sin facultades para satisfacerlos y sin poder para reprimirlos los refirió al Sr Gob.^{r} mismo en Santa Fé esperando q. este S͞or. tendria el tino y fuerza de caracter suficiente para efectuar lo mismo q. hallaba tan malo, no pudieron egecutar los inermes subalternos á quienes lo habia repetidas veces ordenado. Llegados ciento y tantos Yutas á Santa Fé y como de constumbre depocitados sus trenes y armas, y la caballada puesta al cuidado dela tropa, *nueve capitancillos* fueron á verse con el Sr Martinez y los demas indios se esparcieron porla ciudad porlas tiendas y casas procurando tratar por lo que nesecitaban. En la vicita que hicieron al Sr Martinez los capitancillos le espucieron sus quejas, y despues de satisfechos de estas de algun modo pasaron á que de constumbre establecida recivian gratificaciones todas las veces q.^{e} por algun motivo ó por solo su querer vicitaban al Gob.^{r} de Nuevo Mejico.

Ala vista de las gratificaciones los capitancillos notaron una grande des-
minucion delo q.^e aconstumbraban recivir, y selo declararon al S^r
Martinez, usando naturalmente de un lenguaje esprecivo de sus senti-
mientos por el q.^e manifestaban que despues de ofendidos seles queria
dar menos q. cuando amigos y sin queja por mera gratificacion y esprecion de su alianza. El Sr Martinez replico un poco en el espiritu en q.^e
havia dictado las ordenes al juez de paz dela frontera, y uno delos capitancillos al querer representarle su injusticia deceando hacer uso de
toda elocuencia la cual conciste entre los Yndios tanto enlas palabras,
como enlas mociones y gestos le dijo entre otras cosas. *"Como siendo de
tierra fuera y tan pobre que nesecitaba delo que el gobierno concedia
álos Yndios aliados venia tan lejos á poner en malos terminos los Yutas
con los Nuevos Mejicos que desde muchas generaciones pasadas vivian
en buena paz é inteligencia."* El Sr Martinez intimidado ó avergonsado
por este reproche tan vivo, y tan natural en los Yndios dió voces que
oidas delas guardias acudieron y por su orden sin embargo deque los
capitancillos estaban desarmados y que pudieron haver sido apresados
y castigados fueron todos barvaram.^te asecinados igualmente que
algunos otros Yndios que se hallaban en las inmediaciones. Al tumulto
de esta matanza los demas Yndios notando ó aprendiendo lo que pasa-
ba corrieron hacia donde havian dejado sus trenes y armas y por temor
delo que les pudiera suseder se retiraron precipitadamente juntos por la
calle principal temiendo ser perceguidos, pero los pocos soldados quelos
siguieron se tubieron siempre á una buena distancia de ellos pues que
despues que se juntaron los Yndios solo se mataron dos Yndios. Al
mismo tiempo que los Yndios bajaban porla calle principal su caballada de ciento cinco vestias conducida porlos soldados entraba ála Plaza
por el callejon de Scolly y se pucieron en el corral de Palacio. Muchas
personas pensaron entonces q. el Sr Martinez dispondria que la tropa
aprovenchando las monturas y vestias de los Yutas los perseguiria hasta
acabarlos puesto que el mismo havia empesado las ostilidades, pero
dho. S^r no lo creyó combeniente aunq. sele advirtió que estando la
rancheria de estos Yutas en Abiquiú hera facil hir, y apoderarse de sus
familias antes q.^e los fugitivos llegasen allá, y por ese medio restablecer
la paz con ellos: pero que si seles daba tiempo ellos sacarian venganza
delas muertes que seles habian hecho en los pobres vecinos de las fronteras que sorprenderian desprevenidos. El Sr Gral. Martinez no creyó
nesesario usar de tanta actividad contra un enemigo despreciable, ni le
pareció combeniente discontinuar los grandes preparativos que estaba
haciendo para una corrida de toros, asi es que ni fué, ni despacho á

nadie contra los Yutas. Sin embargo dela firme determinacion q.ᵉ este Sʳ havia tomado se esforsaba en tran quilisar algunos delos vecinos que le manifestaron algun cuidado por las jurisdicciones de arriba, asegurandoles que los Yutas hirian huyendo lejos sin descansar y que despues aunq. se reunieran en grandes numeros no heran capaces de tomar la ofensiba y mucho menos de tomar á Santa Fé et.ª [etcétera] errando completamente sobre lo primero y diciendo una nesedad sobre lo segundo porq. Santa Fé ademas de ser uno de los pocos puntos centricos del Departamento tiene de guarnicion toda la tropa del Paiz. Al mismo tiempo que el Sōr. Martinez estaba todo ocupado de sus toros, dela seguridad de Santa Fé y dela de su apreciable persona, los Yutas estaban sacrificando casi al capricho los mas respectables ciudadanos de Abiquiú. Entre los victimas que por la culpable torpedad del Sōr. Martinez sucumbieran en la demarcacion de Abiquiú permitanme VV. Señores, que haga mencion honorable delos capitanes Vigil y Salazar porq. ambos habian rendido servicios importantes ála Patria, y porq. ambos sucumbieron como los valientes despues de muy acuchillado el pecho. Ni cuando la noticia delas muertes q. cometieron los Yutas en Abiquiú llegó á Santa Fé, tomó el Sʳ Martinez medida alguna para proteger las fronteras; todo su conato se dirigia ála seguridad de su persona y de su mando q. sus allegados le habian hecho entender que peligraba; pues le aseguraban q. tanto venida el lenguage q. usaron con el y los recientes ultrages delos Yutas enlas fronteras heran obra de sus enemigos que los empleaban con el obgeto de distraherlo y sorprenderlo si despachaba la tropa. Sin embargo á fuerza de representaciones que sele hicieron hiso un esfuerso sobre si mismo y despacho un corto destacamento álos Pueblos de Abiquiú, Rito y Ojo Caliente.

El Gῑal. Martinez no se distinguió solamente por su grande inorancia, de nuestra cituacion y relaciones con las tribus gentiles que nos avecinan, pero manifestó tambien que inoraba ó que voluntariamente descuidaba las macsimas mas tribiales dela milicia, cual entre otras, la de aniquilar al enemigo ó sacar de él la mayor ventaja pocible puesto q. la havia tomado el mismo muy decidida; pero no, por su fatal inorancia de nuestra cituacion ó por su falsa delicadeza sobre la esprecion inconciderada de un infeliz barvaro nos ha abierto una guerra sangrienta con una tribú valiente y aguerrida, con quien haviamos estado desde tiempo inmemorial en terminos de amistad tan intima que en muchas ocaciones los Yutas como auciliares nuestros hán vertido su sangre generosamente á nuestro lado combatiendo los enemigos del Nuevo

Mejico. Fue tanta la preocupacion del S͞r Martinez sobre el peligro de una rebolucion contra su adm͞on. en la cual los Yutas tomaban parte, q. cuando alguno le incinuaba lo combeniente de hacer marchar fuerzas contra los Yutas tenia siempre la devilidad de querer persuadir q.ᵉ el punto de peligro hera Santa Feé, y que en cuanto álos Yutas él los castigaria rigurosamente enla primavera, llebandoles la guerra á sus hogares, y esplicando sobre esto sus planes de campaña y las maniobras q. intentaba hacer para vencerlos, sin reparar q. todos sus grandes imaginados movimientos si debian verificarse en las tierras delos Yutas seria en cierras tan escabrosas enlas q.ᵉ no hay mas veredas que las que hacen los carneros cimarrones y los conejos. En fin mientras mas se esforsaba en justificar su inaccion y sus esperanzas, mas se ridiculisaba, porq. todo Nuevo Mejico sabe por esperiencia que enlas guerras con los gentiles, ecepto las marchas secretas y la comvinacion de los ataques, lo demas del combate depende siempre de los esfuersos personales delos individuos sin mas regla ni tatica que la virtud marcial particular de cada uno.

Al mismo tiempo que el S͞r Martínez comprometia tan fuertemente la seguridad del Departamento creandonos enemigos esteriores, tambien por otro lado fomentaba un descontento entre sus havitantes que si hubiera durado algun tiempo mas su administracion hubiera ácaso acarreado algun desorden: Ello es que sea por devilidad ó con todo propocito para. q. remediaran sus nesecidades sus favoritos autoriso q. se practicaran ciertas arbitrariedades por medios tan ilegales que solo la humildad, y falta de recursos delos mas que los padecian las pudieron dejar pasar tan tranquilamente. Referiré algunas delas principales. 1ª Un vecino de Taos que habia de hecho pensado matado á otro arrastrandolo de un braso á cabesa de silla hulló del Paiz para evitar el castigo q.ᵉ le esperaba, el año de 1844. bolvió y luego q. llegó fue puesto preso en la carcel de esta ciudad, de donde salió sin que se supiese los medios deque se valió la gobernacion para justificarlo, el caso es que, el uso sin duda de un lenguaje tan persuacivo con el S͞r Martinez, y conlos S͞res. que le aconcejaban, que sin forma de juicio ni sentencia absolutoria de ningun tribunal competente fué absuelto el reo q. bolvió luego á su casa donde vive desde entonces á pesar delos pesares, gosando de tanta tranquilidad como cualesquiera otro hombre honrado é inocente. 2ª A solicitud de sus favoritos concintió el S͞r Martinez q. las propiedades de un Americano asecinado en la frontera de este Departam.ᵗᵒ cuyos matadores havian sido descubiertos y perceguidos en justicia, á instancia del consul Americano, y cuyas propiedades habian sido yá puestas ála dispocicion de ese Señor, y sobre cuyo asunto tubo una larga correspondencia conla gobernacion fueron *ostenciblemente* investidas á favor de los fondos publicos ó de su bolcillo. Esponiendo asi por veneficios privados este Departamento y la Republica á que algun dia los Estados Unidos hagan cargos fundados sobre una injusticia tan chocante.

El Gr̄al. Martinez tubo la suerte de q.ᵉ las diferentes carabanas q. llegaron delos Estados Unidos rindieran en el tiempo de su adm̄on. mas delo q. habian hecho los años anteriores, y de que los dr̄os. [derechos] de esportacion para los mismos subieran tambien á una suma conciderable. Ademas de esto se estableció en su tp̄o. [tiempo] un impuesto sobre los efectos que venian del interior de la Republica, y uso este Sʳ tanto del credito q. le daba su cituacion que recibió prestados delos Sr̄es. capitalistas del Rio Abajo, sumas conciderables; y á pesar de todas estas ventajas de q. carecieron sus anteserores la tropa por falta de regularidad de sus pagas manifestó en varias ocaciones su descontento y su disciplina y subordinacion decayeron notablemente. Al mismo tiempo que la tropa sufria grandes privaciones y q. las mas de sus pagas las recivian en renglones q. no les heran utiles, ó cuyo uso le es prohivido por ordenanza como lo son las varajas y el aguardiente, algunos favoritos recivian sus sueldos adelantados por muchos meces. Por este manejo se creó el Sōr. Martinez, una fama no embidiable entre las personas de responsabilidad, y sea que en concecuencia de este manejo se vaciaran las cajas nacionales y sele acabara el credito, ello és q. manifestó despues unos apuros, que ápesar dela pobresa general del Paiz pocas ocaciones hemos visto semejantes. Entonces fué cuando mando fuertem.ᵗᵉ dela influencia quele daba su pocicion en este Departam.ᵗᵒ, y particularm.ᵗᵉ con los mas delos Señores Vocales de esta Honorable Asamblea conciguio con pretestos de imbaciones de Tejanos y de Yndios q. esta misma Honorable Asamblea decretará contrario á Ley á constumbre, y á combeniencia un emprestito forsoso que fue llevado á efecto en el modo mas absurdo y arvitrario pocible. La clase contribuyente no estaba representada: Las cuotas fueron señaladas al capricho, sin vase sobre el capital y sin regla alguna. Un vecino declarado estrangero pocos dias antes de darse el dicho Decreto fue cuotado con 600. pesos y por haver representado sus dr̄os. fue puesto enla carcel publica. Los encargados delas tiendas en Santa Fé, de algunos Sr̄es. del Rio Abajo cuotados en el prestamo forsoso y q. reusaron pagarlos enlos lugares de su recidencia fueron tambien puestos en la carcel y al fin obligados á dejar q.ᵉ el encargado del Sʳ

Martinez se pagara enlas d$\overline{\text{has}}$. tiendas de lo q.^{e} seles ecsigia á sus dueños ausentes. Enla jurisdicion de Taos, dos delos individuos comprendidos en el prestamo el uno en cama y el otro austente se sospechó por no pagarlo fueron perceguidos como si fueran peores q. criminales de lesa Nacion pues q. hicieron venir el hijo de uno de ellos desde San Fernando de Taos al Rio Arriba para q. respondiera y pagará por su padre. Por este espiritu de arvitrariedad y de ecsacion se enemistó el Sr Martinez con todos los comerciantes nativos y estrangeros y fue causa tambien q. ademas del vecino q. el mismo extrangeró, otro dela misma Nacion y clase representará con el primero al Ministro de S.M.B. de quien nacieron vasallos sobre las injusticias q. padecieron, y que el Supremo haya tomado ambos casos en concideracion.

El Sr Martinez despues de causar al Nuevo Mejico los perjuicios, se retiró por dispocicion del Supremo Gobierno á gosar delas dulsuras dela vida privada, quedando deviendo en este Departam.^{to} segun se asegura crecidas sumas á diferentes individuos entre otras una de 18.000. pesos á D. Antonio Sandoval. No dudo que esto junto con sus medidas administratibas perpetuaran, pero no ventajosamente su memoria.

Al S^r G$\overline{\text{ral}}$. Martinez le susedió en el mando militar el Sr D. Fran.^{co} Garcia Conde como G$\overline{\text{ral}}$. en Gefe dela 5ª Division. Este S^r duró muy poco tiempo entre nosotros para q. pudieramos apreciar devidamente todas su buenas cualidades las que debemos suponer abundan en su caracter. Pero á pesar de su corta visita no pudimos menos de notar que por algun error sin duda dió pasos en el Nuevo Mejico que no dieron favorable opinion de sus principios. Apenas llegó se puso en competencia conla autoridad politica y con los empleados de Hacienda por querer asumir facultades que no le correspondian, y q. á pesar de la concideracion q. todos generalmente en el Nuevo Mejico le tenian por su alta graduacion creyeron justo los atacados de recistirle. Una de sus medidas en lo militar lo desprestijió enteramente con esta clase de venemeritos ciudadanos q. fué el haver elevado á un ranchero honrrado pero inorante, de oficial de auciliares dela Patria ála Comand.^{a} P$\overline{\text{ra}}$l. [Principal] de Nuevo Mejico sobre un crecido numero de oficiales veteranos y uno de ellos de alta graduacion. El Sr Garcia Conde á pesar dela recistencia que encontró enlas autoridades Politica y de Hacienda tubo modo de conceguir apoderarse de una fuerte suma de dinero q. estaba enlas cajas Nacionales destinada en parte para pagar el emprestito forsoso, arrancadola delas manos del Tesorero por la fuerza, en cuyo caso y para efectuar su decignio puso preso á este empleado. El emprestito forsoso estaba asegurado con la fé publica, la solemne promesa dela governacion, y dela Honorable Asamblea, y fué en vano que se le representó lo vergonsoso q. hera faltar ála fé en semejantes contratos; dicho S^r incisitió en su propocito y con pretesto de querer comprar monturas y remonta para los Precidiales de Nuevo Mejico, y con pretesto tambien de conducir estos dos articulos se llevo dos oficiales que de algun modo havian contrariado sus miras como vocales dela Honorable Asamblea. Todos V.V. S$\overline{res}$. saben que los dos oficiales hán regresado á Santa Fé y q. no han traido ni las monturas ni la caballada mencionadas, y q. yá no hay ni esperanzas de que nunca nos venga. El Sr Garcia Conde tubo la vondad antes de dejarnos de favorecer al Nuevo Mejico con suspender de sus funciones álos empleados de Hacienda q. merecieron la confianza del Supremo Gobierno para encargarlos al Sr Comandante Militar antes referido y calificado.

Es sobre estos hechos Señores que fundo mi opinion para decear que los mandos politico y militar sean dados á nativos ó avecindados en el Departamento para que estando penetrados de nuestros intereces y de nuestros deceos, aun suponiendo q. no sean dotados de talentos muy elevados los que se nombren para ellos, nos ahorren álo menos las vicicitudes que los S$\overline{res}$. Perez, Martinez, y Garcia Conde nos hán causado.

Concluyo pues proponiendo ála Honorable Asamblea que dirija instrucciones á nuestro digno representante en el Congreso dela Union D. Tomas Chavez y Castiyo para que solicite dela autoridad competente q. los mandos politico y militar de este Departamento, sean siempre concedidos á personas q. hayan recidido bastante tiempo entre nosotros para conoser intimamente nuestra cituacion, y nuestros verdaderos intereces.

Santa Fé Junio 22. 1846.
Donaciano Vigil [signature]

Notes

Introduction

1 Josiah Gregg, *Commerce of the Prairies*, Max L. Moorhead, ed. (1st ed., 1844; Norman: University of Oklahoma Press, 1954); George W. Kendall, *Narrative of the Texan Santa Fe Expedition*, 2 vols. (New York: Harper & Brothers, 1844); James Josiah Webb, *Adventures in the Santa Fe Trade, 1844-1847*, Ralph P. Bieber, ed. (Glendale, Ca.: Arthur H. Clark Co., 1931); Alfred S. Waugh, *Travels in Search of the Elephant: The Wanderings of Alfred S. Waugh, Artist, in Louisiana, Missouri, and Santa Fe, in 1845-1846*, John Francis McDermott, ed. (St. Louis: Missouri Historical Society, 1951); and A. Wislizenus, *Memoir of a Tour to Northern Mexico* (1st ed., 1848; Albuquerque: Calvin Horn, Publisher, 1969). At the time of the American invasion a substantial group of foreigners visited New Mexico and described local conditions. Among them were the authors of two classic accounts: Susan Shelby Magoffin, whose diary, edited by Stella M. Drumm, was published under the title *Down the Santa Fe Trail and into Mexico* (1st ed., 1926; New Haven: Yale University Press, 1926), and Lewis Garrard, *Wah-to-yah and the Taos Trail* (1st ed., 1850; Palo Alto, Ca.: American West Publishing Co., 1968). A number of studies examine the prejudice and shallowness inherent in these travel accounts, but see especially: Cecil Robinson, *Mexico and the Hispanic Southwest in American Literature* (Tucson: University of Arizona Press, 1977), and Janet Lecompte, "Manuel Armijo and the Americans," *Journal of the West*, 19 (July 1980), pp. 51-63.

2 The most notable other exceptions are in H. Bailey Carroll and J. Villasana Haggard, trans. & eds. *Three New Mexico Chronicles: The* Exposición *of Don Pedro Bautista Pino, 1812; the* Ojeada *of Lic. Antonio Barreiro, 1832; and the additions by Don José Agustín de Escudero, 1849* (Albuquerque: Quivira Society, 1942), and in David J. Weber, ed., *Northern Mexico on the Eve of the United States Invasion: Rare Imprints Concerning California, Arizona, New Mexico, and Texas, 1821-1846* (New York: Arno Press, 1976).

3 Comandante General del Departamento de Nuevo Mejico [Manuel Armijo], to the troops under his command, Santa Fe, June 6, 1846. Donaciano Vigil Papers, New Mexico State Records Center and Archives, Santa Fe, New Mexico (NMSRCA). Daniel Tyler, "Governor Armijo's Moment of Truth," *Journal of the West*, 11 (April 1972), p. 311.

4 David M. Pletcher, *The Diplomacy of Annexation: Texas, Oregon, and the Mexican War* (Columbia: University of Missouri Press, 1973), pp. 286-91, 354-55, & 384-86; David J. Weber, *The Mexican Frontier, 1821-1846: The American Southwest Under Mexico* (Albuquerque: University of New Mexico Press, 1982), p. 272; Lansing B. Bloom, "New Mexico Under Mexican Administration, 1821-1846," *Old Santa Fe*, 2 (April 1915), pp. 352-53, translates a circular from Governor Armijo, dated June 6, 1846, which discusses some of these matters. Dwight L. Clarke, *Stephen Watts Kearny: Soldier of the West* (Norman: University of Oklahoma Press, 1961), pp. 113-15.

5 Journal of the Departmental Assembly, June 18, 1846, Mexican Archives of New Mexico (MANM), NMSRCA, microfilm edition, r. 42, fr. 861. For the size and membership of the Assembly at this time, see Ward Alan Minge, "Frontier Problems in New Mexico Preceding the Mexican War, 1840-1846" (Ph.D. diss., University of New Mexico, 1965), p. 325, and Lansing B. Bloom, "New Mexico Under Mexican Administration, 1821-1846," *Old Santa Fe*, 2 (January 1915), p. 252.

6 Another draft of this document, unsigned and dated May 16, 1846, is in the Ritch Papers, no. 231, Huntington Library, San Marino, California. The document at the Huntington may, of course, be misdated.

7 Vigil's analysis seems sound. American traders made a similar impact on Mexican-Indian relations all across the West, from Louisiana to California. See Weber, *Mexican Frontier*, pp. 83-105.

8 Antonio José Martínez, *Espocisión que el presbítero Antonio José Martínez, cura de Taos de Nuevo México, dirije al Gobierno del Exmo. Sor. General Antonio López de Santa Anna. Proponiedo la civilisación de las naciones bárbaras que son al contorno del Departamento de Nuevo México* (Taos: J. M. B., 1843), reproduced in facsimile in Weber, ed., *Northern Mexico*.

9 Donaciano Vigil to Armijo, June 30, 1846, quoted in Howard Roberts Lamar, *The Far Southwest, 1846-1912: A Territorial History* (New Haven: Yale University Press, 1966), p. 60.

10 The quotation is from the Journal of the Assembly, June 18, 1846. A statement at the end of one copy of the Vigil proposal, signed by José Chávez, president of the Assembly, and Miguel E. Pino, and dated June 18, 1846, indicated that the Assembly authorized the sending of the two copies (MANM, r. 42, fr. 339).

11 An incomplete copy, written in a beautiful hand and addressed to the "Soberano Congreso," is in the Donaciano Vigil Papers, NMSRCA, suggesting the possibility that the document was not transcribed in time to send to Mexico City.

12 Journal of the Departmental Assembly, June 22, 1846, MANM, r. 42, fr. 893.

13 Carlos María Bustamante, *El Gabinete mexicano durante el segundo período de la administración del Exmo. Señor Presidente Anastasio Bustamante*, 2 vols. (Mexico: Imprenta de Jose M. Lara, 1842), I: 36. Bustamante based his account on the official reports of Governor Armijo.

14 Armijo to the Ministro de Guerra y Marina, Oct. 11, 1837, in *Diario del Gobierno*, Nov. 30, 1837, quoted in Weber, *The Mexican Frontier*, p. 263. Philip Reno, "Rebellion in New Mexico — 1837," *New Mexico Historical Review*, 40 (July 1965), p. 197, correctly points out that most sources are very critical of the rebels because extant accounts of the rebellion come largely from their victorious opponents. Fray Angélico Chávez, *But Time and Chance: The Story of Padre Martínez of Taos, 1793-1867* (Santa Fe: Sunstone Press, 1981), pp. 51-59, seems to endorse the view of those contemporaries who saw the revolt an expression of "resentment among the lower social and economic classes" (p. 52).

15 W. G. Ritch, "Governor Donaciano Vigil," Santa Fe *Weekly New Mexican*, August 28, 1877; Reno, "Rebellion in New Mexico," p. 105. Depositions regarding the loyalty of Vigil in the insurrection of August 1837, January 2-4, 1838, Ritch Papers, no. 169. Fresh information regarding the 1837 rebellion and José Gonzales is in Janet Lecompte's book, *Rebellion in Río Arriba, 1837* (Albuquerque: University of New Mexico Press, 1985).

16 Donaciano Vigil, "A Statement Concerning Historical Events Between 1801 and 1851," Ritch Papers, no. 482. Vigil apparently made this statement about 1851. Samuel Ellison translated it into English.

17 Minge, "Frontier Problems," p. 280.

18 For an outline of the distinguished career of García Conde (1804-1849), see the *Diccionario Porrúa: Historia, Biografía y Geografía de México*, 2 vols, (3rd ed.; Mexico: Editorial Porrúa, 1970), I: 822.

19 Bloom, "New Mexico Under Mexican Administration," 2: 241, 357. Weber, *Mexican Frontier*, p. 108.

20 Little information pertaining to García Conde exists in the secondary literature. For his negotiations with the Comanches, see Minge, "Frontier Problems," pp. 294-96.

21 Journal of the Assembly, June 22, 1846, MANM, r. 42, fr. 893.

22 Journal of the Assembly, June 29, 1846 and July 7, 1846, MANM, r. 42, frs. 896-97.

23 W. G. Ritch published an article-length biography of Vigil shortly after his death: "Governor Donaciano Vigil," Santa Fe *Weekly New Mexican*, August 28, 1877; Ralph Emerson Twitchell copied much of Ritch's article, without attribution, in his *History of the Military Occupation of the Territory of New Mexico from 1846 to 1851* (Denver: Smith-Brooks Co., 1909), pp. 207-08; and F. Stanley [Francis L. Stanley Crocchiola] has written a book-length biography, *Giant in Lilliput: The Story of Donaciano Vigil* (Pampa, Texas: Pampa Print Shop, 1963). Stanley's biography is built on archival research as well as a reading of published sources, but contains no notes, is badly organized, and should be used with caution. For the biographies of other Mexican frontiersmen, see Weber, *Northern Mexico*, pp. 387-88.

24 James Conklin, quoted in Ritch, "Vigil."

25 Much of the information from this paragraph has been gleaned from Crocchiola, *Giant*, and Ritch, "Vigil." Both authors agree on most of these details. For Vigil as secretary of the Assembly, newspaper publisher, and merchant, see Bloom, "New Mexico Under Mexican Administration," 2: 165-67, 230, 234, 236.

26 Ralph Emerson Twitchell, *Leading Facts of New Mexico History*, 2 vols. (Cedar Rapids, Iowa: Torch Press, 1912), II: 214.

27 Report of the Citizens of New Mexico to the President of Mexico, Santa Fe, September 26, 1846, in Max L. Moorhead, ed. and trans., "Notes and Documents," *New Mexico Historical Review*, 26 (January 1951), p. 75. In his "Statement Concerning Historical Events," written ca. 1851, Ritch Papers, Vigil again placed blame on Armijo.

28 Vigil to "Fellow Citizens," Santa Fe, January 22, 1847, quoted in Twitchell, *Leading Facts*, II: 248-49. For the formation of civilian government in September 1847, see ibid., p. 214.

29 Robert W. Larson, *New Mexico's Quest for Statehood, 1848-1912* (Albuquerque: University of New Mexico Press, 1968), p. 8.

30 *The Legislative Blue-Book of the Territory of New Mexico*, W. G. Ritch, comp. (Santa Fe: Charles W. Greene, 1882), pp. 102, 105, 109, 110.

31 Vigil's role in land manipulation has been brought to light by Em Hall, "Giant Before the Surveyor-General: The Land Career of Donaciano Vigil," in John R. and Christine M. Van Ness, eds., *Spanish and Mexican Land Grants in New Mexico and Colorado* (Manhattan, Kansas: Sunflower University Press, 1980), pp. 64-73.

32 Lamar, *Far Southwest*, p. 65. The laudatory characterizations appear in Ritch, "Vigil," written shortly after Vigil's death.

33 After completing my editing of these documents, I learned that Janet Lecompte has included her own translation of a portion of Vigil's proposal of June 22, in which he discusses Governor Albino Pérez, in her book, *Rebellion in Río Arriba, 1837*.

Part I

1 An unsigned copy of this document, dated May 16, 1846, is in the Ritch Collection, Huntington Library, San Marino, California. It may be an early draft, or it may have been misdated. My transcription and translation are taken from a signed copy dated June

18, 1846, in the Donaciano Vigil Papers, New Mexico State Records Center and Archives, Santa Fe, New Mexico (NMSRCA). This document was integrated into the Mexican Archives of New Mexico (MANM) and is available on the forty-two roll microfilm series, MANM, r. 41, frs. 330-339. The Huntington and NMSRCA versions are essentially the same. I have used the Huntington copy to clarify poorly written words or to fill in blanks where portions of the NMSRCA are torn.

2 General Mariano Martínez de Lejanza (1844-45), of whom Vigil has more to say in his proposal of June 22.

3 Vigil used the terms *bárbaros* (barbarians) and *gentiles* (heathens) when referring to Indians who pillage and murder. He seldom used the more general term *indio* (Indian) because he, like other Mexicans on the frontier, distinguished between Indians such as the Pueblos, who had become Christianized and who maintained peaceful relations with Mexicans, and Indians who retained customs that he regarded as "heathen" or "barbaric."

4 Vigil used the term "ganados mayor y menor," meaning to include sheep and goats as well as cattle and horses. I have translated this simply as livestock.

5 Vigil uses the term "Señor" on this occasion, addressing himself in the singular, apparently to the head of the Assembly. Later on in this document, he addresses himself to the entire Assembly, using "Señores." It seems appropriate to maintain the plural form consistently.

6 Raid and counterraid characterized Mexican relations with several of the tribes in New Mexico, but the elderly may have been recalling the relative peace that came to New Mexico following the signing of peace treaties with Comanches in 1785-86. See Marc Simmons, ed. and trans., *Border Comanches: Seven Spanish Colonial Documents, 1785-1819* (Santa Fe: Stagecoach Press, 1967), pp. 13-15.

7 The Huntington Library version of the manuscript contains the term "tierra fuera" but this was crossed out and replaced with "el interior."

8 A special fund for gifts to Indians continued to be used in the Mexican period, but it was not as large as that of the colonial period and Vigil considered it less effective. See Weber, *The Mexican Frontier, 1821-1846: The American Southwest Under Mexico* (Albuquerque: University of New Mexico Press, 1982), p. 105.

9 The Arroyo de don Carlos was apparently the site of a Spanish massacre of a Comanche trading party, September 28, 1774, led by don Carlos Fernández. For the battle and its context, see Elizabeth A. H. John, *Storms Brewed in Other Men's Worlds* (College Station: Texas A&M Press, 1975), pp. 477-79. In a play, "Los Comanches," New Mexicans continued to sing the victory of "don Carlos" well into the 20th century, although the historical facts had become muddled. See John Donald Robb, *Hispanic Folk Music of New Mexico and the Southwest: A Self-Portrait of a People* (Norman: University of Oklahoma Press, 1980), p. 602. The place itself is today called Don Carlos Creek, in Union County. T. M. Pearce, ed., *New Mexico Place Names: A Geographical Dictionary* (Albuquerque: University of New Mexico Press, 1965), p. 48. In 1850, the American artist Richard Kern did two drawings of the "Arroyo de Don Carlos" as he traveled west over the Santa Fe Trail beyond Round Mound and Point of Rocks. Kern Sketchbook D, private collection of Fred W. Cron.

The campaign of "orejas del Conejo," apparently took place in 1717. Old timers later remembered it incorrectly as a turning point in New Mexico relations with Comanches. Amado Chaves, writing in the early 1900s, thought that the battle had "ended the wars between the Spanish settlers and the Comanches for all time. Whenever the young bucks wanted to start a war against the Spaniards the grey haired old men would take them to las 'Orejas del Conejo' . . . and show to them the pile of bones and skulls." Chaves, "The Defeat of the Comanches in 1717," *Historical Society of New Mexico, [Publication] no. 8* (Santa Fe: New Mexico Printing Co., 1906), p. 9. Chaves and Vigil exaggerated the importance of the battle. See Oakah L. Jones, Jr., *Pueblo Warriors & Spanish Conquest* (Norman: University of Oklahoma Press, 1966), p. 96-97. The tradition that Amado Chaves had learned put the site of the battle in what is today West Texas, but more likely it occurred not far from the Arroyo de don Carlos along the Santa Fe Trail near Rabbit Ears Mountain, six miles north of present Clayton, New Mexico. Pearce, *New Mexico Place Names*, p. 128.

10 Vigil's report on the success of Spanish policy is overdrawn, but he was not the only officer on the northern frontier to recall the past in wistfully romantic terms. See Ignacio Zúñiga, *Rápida ojeada al estado de Sonora* (Mexico: Juan Ojeda, 1835), pp. 15, 22. This rare pamphlet is reproduced in Weber, ed., *Northern Mexico on the Eve of the United States Invasion. Rare Imprints . . .* (New York: Arno Press, 1976).

11 The best single-volume discussion of this trade is Max L. Moorhead, *New Mexico's Royal Road: Trade and Travel on the Chihuahua Trail* (Norman: University of Oklahoma Press, 1958).

12 Vigil describes Baca (1823-1825) as "Gefe Político del Departamento." Here, Vigil is making a distinction between the offices of civil and military head of New Mexico, which were usually occupied by the same man. Baca held just one position. New Mexico was not a "department" in Baca's time. After the adoption of the 1824 Constitution, it had become a territory.

13 Vigil may have remembered these events, since he was in his early twenties when they occurred. Or he may have read about them in Josiah Gregg's *Commerce of the Prairies*, first published in 1844. See the modern edition, Max L. Moorhead, ed. (Norman: University of Oklahoma Press, 1954), p. 160. Vigil's understanding of these arrangements made by Baca seems correct. See Weber, *The Taos Trappers: The Fur Trade in the Far Southwest, 1540-1846* (Norman: University of Oklahoma Press, 1971), pp. 66, 67, 79, 87.

14 A *quintal* was the equivalent of 100 Spanish *libras*, roughly equal to 100 pounds. The *peso duro* was a silver peso, roughly equal to a dollar in Vigil's day. Vigil's figures seem on the high side, but since trapping beavers by foreigners was illegal after 1824, considerable smuggling occurred and no reliable statistics exist. Vigil's figures of 160 quintales would have equalled 160,000 pounds, or 320 packs of beaver. This would have been worth $100,000, as he claimed, only at eastern prices (not St. Louis or Santa Fe prices), when beaver sold at $6 a pound. In 1826, James Baird complained to the Mexican government that $100,000 worth of beaver fur had been smuggled out of New Mexico; the figure may have become part of the region's folklore. Weber, *Taos Trapper*, pp. 118, 206-07.

15 Here Vigil seems to be describing efforts by some New Mexico officials to raise tariffs to protect Mexican manufacturers and merchants, and to preserve the dwindling population of beaver from American trappers. See Moorhead, *New Mexico's Royal Road*, chapter 6, and Weber, *Taos Trappers*, chapters 7 & 8, for examples of episodes that Vigil deplored.

16 There is no evidence to corroborate Vigil's suggestion that Baca was relieved of his office (in September 1825) because he was not stern enough with foreigners. Actually, Baca's successor, Antonio Narbona, continued Baca's policy of granting trapping licenses to foreigners, but opposition to foreign trappers began to harden during his term (1825-1827). Lansing B. Bloom, "New Mexico Under Mexican Administration,

1822-1846," *Old Santa Fe*, I (January 1914), p. 244. Weber, *Taos Trappers*, pp. 95, 105-06.

17 Vigil is referring to trading posts, established by Americans on the north side of the Arkansas — the international border according to the Adams-Onís Treaty of 1819. The 1830s saw the establishment of a number of these posts, Bent's Fort being the most successful. The traders apparently moved north to avoid enforcement of Mexican laws, as Vigil suggests, but they also moved out onto the Plains to capture the trade in buffalo hides that was supplanting the dwindling supply of beaver fur in that decade. See Weber, *Taos Trappers*, chapter 13.

18 See above, n. 17. Vigil uses the Spanish name "Chato" for the Platte, and "Colorado" for the Red, but he used "Arcansas" for the Arkansas, instead of "Napestle," which Spaniards had long used for that river.

19 In maintaining that most of the inhabitants of New Mexico were armed only with bows and arrows, Vigil is probably not exaggerating. See Weber, *Mexican Frontier*, p. 120. A few months later, on September 26, 1846, a letter to the president of Mexico, signed by 105 New Mexicans, including Vigil, stated that New Mexico could have resisted American forces if Governor Armijo had "arranged in time for the production of munitions of war, for which there was more than enough powder and lead in the Department." Quoted in Max L. Moorhead, ed. and trans., "Notes and Documents," *New Mexico Historical Review*, 26 (July 1951), p. 74. The same letter also suggests that there were sufficient guns.

20 Here, Vigil touched upon a long-standing problem. A dozen years earlier, Governor Francisco Sarracino had published a decree in which he criticized well-to-do New Mexicans for putting responsibility for defense in the hands of the poor. Weber, *Mexican Frontier*, p. 117.

21 Restrictions on the importation of arms and a prohibition on the importation of munitions had been in effect since 1840, if not before. Ward Alan Minge, "Frontier Problems in New Mexico Preceding the Mexican War, 1840-1846" (Ph.D. diss., University of New Mexico, 1965), pp. 114-15.

22 Vigil uses the term "hijos del paiz," meaning literally "sons of the country." The "country" he has in mind here, however, is clearly New Mexico — not Mexico.

23 The version of this document in MANM, transcribed here, contains an error when it says: "Como no lo aseguran." The "no" does not seem to belong.

Part III

1 My transcript and translation of this document derives from a signed copy in the Ritch Collection (no. 233), Huntington Library, San Marino, California. An unsigned copy, also dated June 22, 1846, is in the Donaciano Vigil Papers, NMSRCA. This document was integrated into the MANM, and is available in the microfilm edition of MANM, r. 41, frs. 340-355.

2 On January 2, 1846, Gen. Mariano Paredes took control of the central government. Vigil may be referring to changes that Paredes, a provisional president, had announced, or to the likelihood of still another government being formed because rumors of a coup were circulating. On July 16, what historian Walter Scholes called the "long awaited revolt" broke out against Paredes and he was overthrown. José Fernando Ramírez, *Mexico Dur-*

ing the War with the United States, Walter V. Scholes, ed., Elliot B. Scherr, trans. (Columbia: University of Missouri Press, 1970), p. 65.

3 Lt. Col. Albino Pérez arrived in New Mexico on June 20, 1835, appointed by Santa Anna to hold simultaneously New Mexico's highest military and civil offices.

4 During Pérez's term in New Mexico the central government was in transition from the federalist, liberal-leaning Constitution of 1824 to the centralist, conservative Constitution of 1836. A territory under the 1824 constitution, New Mexico became a department in 1836. Pérez oversaw the transition. Lansing B. Bloom, "New Mexico Under Mexican Administration, 1821-1846," Old Santa Fe, 2 (July 1914), pp. 3-6. David J. Weber, The Mexican Frontier, 1821-1846: The American Southwest Under Mexico (Albuquerque: University of New Mexico Press, 1982), pp. 31-37.

5 Vigil was almost certainly referring to the Pueblo Revolt of 1680.

6 The Pérez campaigns against Navajos are described in Frank McNitt, Navajo Wars: Military Campaigns, Slave Raids, and Reprisals (Albuquerque: University of New Mexico Press, 1972), pp. 75-79. In the fall of 1836, Pérez took the largest group ever assembled to invade the Navajo country (some 6,000 men), and a few months later he personally led an unusual winter campaign that McNitt termed "perhaps the most difficult undertaken against the Navajos until that time" (p. 77). Both campaigns drained resources and kept volunteers from tending to their own affairs. The latter resulted in considerable suffering from frostbite by Pérez's forces, who might well have been disgruntled by the meager results of the campaign. Navajo raids continued. If Pérez allowed himself to be lulled into a false sense of victory by Navajo negotiators, as Vigil charged, he was not the first, nor would he be the last.

7 The Santa Fe trade was the major source of revenue for the New Mexico government, and embezzlement by customs officials was not unusual. Weber, Mexican Frontier, pp. 149-53.

8 Vigil believed that the upper class was behind the revolt; others have argued that leadership came from the lower class. See ibid., pp. 261-66.

9 On August 8, 1837, near the pueblo of San Ildefonso, rebels routed Pérez's small force. Pérez was beheaded. The others, whom Vigil identifies as murdered, were Pérez's secretary, Jesús María Alarid, District Judge Santiago Abreú, and Santiago's brother Ramón, the local prefect. Ibid., p. 262.

10 Vigil's reference here is to Bustamante's El Gabinete mexicano. See above, Introduction, n. 13.

11 Vigil's reference to the "Texan expedition" is to the effort of a small group sent by the independent Republic of Texas in 1841 to foment rebellion in New Mexico. Armijo handily defeated the hapless Texans and became a national hero. Weber, Mexican Frontier, pp. 266-68.

12 Martínez received the appointment of Commanding General of New Mexico on October 16, 1844, replacing Manuel Armijo in that position. Martínez probably arrived in Santa Fe on December 8, as Vigil says. On December 9 he issued a proclamation to New Mexicans from Santa Fe. Ward Alan Minge, "Frontier Problems in New Mexico Preceding the Mexican War, 1840-1846" (Ph.D. diss., University of New Mexico, 1965), pp. 151, 160, 165. Vigil is correct in saying that the Assembly recommended Martínez and that he occupied the governorship on May 15, 1844. Minge, "Frontier Problems," pp. 188-89.

13 Martínez appears to have had genuine interest in reform: he established a newspaper, La Verdad, replaced a number of judges whom he accused of negligence or corrup-

tion, interested himself in primary education, planted trees in the plaza, and enforced pro-
tectionist laws to keep foreigners out of the retail trade and prevent them from obtaining
large concessions of land. Minge, "Frontier Problems," pp. 208, 210, 216, 220-26. Many
californios also believed that Mexicans from central Mexico saw themselves as superior to
the frontiersmen. Weber, *Mexican Frontier*, p. 241.

14 "Little" or minor chiefs.

15 Correspondence regarding this incident occupies the first three pages of the Santa Fe
newspaper *La Verdad*, September 12, 1844 (copy in the Huntington Library, San Marino,
Ca.). Historian Ward Alan Minge has examined this episode in a chapter published from
his dissertation: "Mexican Independence and a Ute Tragedy in Santa Fe, 1844," in Albert
Schroeder, ed., *Changing Ways of Southwestern Indians: A Historic Perspective*
(Glorieta, N.M.: Rio Grande Press, 1973), pp. 107-22. Martínez blamed the Utes for
becoming unruly in his office and attacking him, causing him to call in the guards. The
episode in Martínez's office occurred on September 6, 1844. Vigil was correct that
Martínez was planning a bullfight at this time, but it was as part of a larger celebration of
Mexico's Independence Day, September 16. Martínez did, as Vigil charged, continue to
make preparations for the bullfight, but he also quickly dispatched troops against the Utes,
contrary to what Vigil claimed.

16 The fight with the Utes that broke out in Martínez's office seems to have marked a
turning point in what had been generally peaceful relations between New Mexicans and
the Utes. It was, therefore, significant enough to merit the attention that Vigil gave it in
this document. Weber, *Mexican Frontier*, p. 93.

17 Vigil is almost certainly referring to the case of Joseph Pulsipher, who was murdered
in November 1840. Pulsipher's personal property was handed over to the American consul
in Santa Fe, Manuel Alvarez, then later reclaimed by New Mexico officials and sold at
auction in July 1844, when Martínez was governor. The case is discussed in Minge, "Frontier Problems," pp. 28-34. Manuel Alvarez, in a letter to the American Secretary of State,
James Buchanan, Independence, Missouri, June 18, 1845, complained about the sale of
Pulsipher's property in terms that Donaciano Vigil later echoed: "Joseph Palsipher [*sic*] an
American Citizen was murdered some years since . . . and his property applied to the
[use] of the public, without any probability of his legal representatives ever having it in
their [power] to receive the least share thereof." Dispatches from United States Consuls in
Santa Fe, 1830-1846, Record Group 59, General Records of the Department of State, National Archives and Records Service, Washington, D.C., File Microcopy no. 199.

18 Vigil's charges against Martínez seem exaggerated. As Martínez pointed out, New
Mexico's treasury was usually empty: "not only is direct taxation not practiced; but neither
[is] indirect taxation all of which, as is well known, supports all governments." Martínez to
the President of the New Mexico Assembly, Santa Fe, August 29, 1844, quoted in Minge,
"Frontier Problems," p. 254. Contrary to Vigil's statement, trade from the United States
appears to have yielded very slender revenues during Martínez's administration. The New
Mexico customs house was closed in the spring and early summer of 1844. Shortly after
becoming governor in May, Martínez had to borrow 12,000 pesos from wealthy citizens.
Not until October did foreign trade bring in revenue, and that was apparently inadequate
to cover the costs of paying the troops and government officials — a perennial problem,
not unique to the administration of Martínez. Minge, "Frontier Problems," pp. 192-94,
200-201, 221-22, 233-38.

19 This was John Scolly ("Juan Scolly"), a British subject and long-time resident of Santa Fe who had married a New Mexico woman and applied for citizenship, but had not yet

received it (Minge, "Frontier Problems," p. 222). Benjamin M. Read, *Illustrated History of New Mexico* (Santa Fe: New Mexican Printing Co., 1912), pp. 412-14, reproduces documents showing that despite Scolly's protestations, he was still a British citizen. He was ordered to pay 600 pesos or have his two stores shut down. If Vigil's account is correct, Scolly went to jail rather than pay the "forced loan." Scolly appealed the decision to the British minister in Mexico City and the matter continued to plague the New Mexico Assembly until the end of 1845. Bloom, "New Mexico Under Mexican Administration," 2 (January 1915), p. 245.

20 Vigil gives a fuller account of this episode than is available elsewhere. Martínez failed to get New Mexicans to pay at all, according to Minge, "Frontier Problems," p. 205, but Vigil's statement here, and his criticism further on in this document of García Conde for appropriating monies earmarked to repay the forced loan, suggest that some people did pay the assessments.

Ironically, Vigil himself was a member of the Assembly that approved the forced loan proposed by Martínez. The Assembly issued a decree on February 14, 1845, requiring payment from twenty-four *capitalistas*, who were assigned designated amounts ranging from 200 to 1,000 pesos each. On May 10, just after Martínez left office, Vigil wrote an elaborate explanation of his vote in the Assembly. Although Vigil opposed the forced loan, he claimed that he voted for it for several reasons. First, he knew that he would be out-voted. Second, he had already incurred the wrath of his fellow assemblymen for opposing another measure. Third, General Martínez was his superior officer and Vigil was already in trouble with the General. Vigil published his explanation, along with supporting documents, in a fourteen-page pamphlet: *Breve esposicion que da al publico el ciudadano Donaciano Vigil, Capitan de la Compañia del Bado, como vocal de la exma. asamblea, manifestando los motivos que le impelieron a votar por el emprestito forzozo que á pedimento del exmo. Sr Gobernador y Comandante Gral. D. Mariano Martinez decretó la misma Honorable Asamblea en 14 de Febrero del corriente año de 1845* ([Santa Fe?]: Imprenta particular a cargo de J. M. B., 1845), copy in the Newberry Library, Chicago, Illinois.

21 Martínez was investigated by the Departmental Assembly for financial mismanagement and charges against him sent to Mexico City. He was apparently removed from office before the case was reviewed. Bloom, "New Mexico Under Mexican Administration," 2 (January 1915), pp. 231-35. On May 1, Martínez turned the governorship over to Mariano Chávez y Castillo, who died on May 16 and was replaced in office by José Chávez. Myra Ellen Jenkins, *Calendar of the Mexican Archives of New Mexico, 1821-1846* (Santa Fe: State of New Mexico Records Center, 1970), p. 129.

22 General Francisco García Conde, *comandante general* of the Fifth Division of the Mexican Army, arrived in Santa Fe toward mid-August, 1845. Changes in the military structure had lowered the title of the ranking military officer in Santa Fe from *comandante general* to *comandante principal*, and made the province more dependent upon Chihuahua — a condition that New Mexicans had previously resented (Jenkins, *Calendar*, pp. 241, 357, and Weber, *Mexican Frontier*, p. 108).

23 The "ignorant rancher" was apparently Juan Andrés Archuleta, who "acted as Comandante General until the middle of August when the Comandancia was centralized in Durango and the office of Comandante General vacated in New Mexico. Archuleta then held the title of Comandante Principal until the spring of 1846." Jenkins, *Calendar*, p. 129. Vigil's characterization of Archuleta is interesting, but his assertion that García Conde appointed him appears to be in error. Juan Andrés Archuleta's son, Diego, was

then serving as New Mexico's delegate to Congress and his influence probably assured his father's high military position. For Diego Archuleta, see Ralph Emerson Twitchell, *The History of the Military Occupation of the Territory of New Mexico from 1846 to 1851* (Denver: Smith-Brooks Co., 1909), pp. 239-48. Vigil's ungracious comment about Archuleta smacks of the envy of an officer passed by for promotion, or perhaps is another effort on Vigil's part to curry favor with Armijo, who is most likely the officer "of high rank" passed over by García Conde.

24 This episode occurred in September 1845, when García Conde insisted that New Mexico's treasurer, Ambrosio Armijo, provide him with funds from the departmental treasury in order to pay the troops that Garcia Conde had brought with him. Armijo refused to do so, and Governor José Chávez ordered Armijo not to deliver public funds to García Conde. Vigil's description of the event seems correct, and reflects the views held by Governor Chávez and a committee of the Department Assembly — both wrote stinging condemnations of García Conde for exceeding his authority and putting himself above the law. Vigil, however, apparently embellished the story. García Conde did not need to put Ambrosio Armijo in jail. He merely threatened to do so if Armijo did not turn the funds over to him within three hours. Armijo, claiming that he suffered from "many illnesses," and that he did not wish to suffer the indignity of going to prison, capitulated before García Conde could carry out his threat. Copies of the angry exchange of letters between García Conde, Armijo, and Governor Chávez are in the Archivo General de la Nación, Mexico, D. F., Ramo de Gobernación, L-1636, E-3, 1845-50.

25 Vigil had firsthand knowledge of this mission. He, along with Antonio Sena, was one of the two members of the Assembly whom García Conde sent to Chihuahua. According to Bloom, both men were presidial captains as well as assemblymen, and the Assembly tried unsuccessfully to keep them in New Mexico to perform their legislative duties. The men left for Chihuahua on October 16, 1845. "New Mexico Under Mexican Administration," 2 (January 1915), pp. 241-42.

26 A shakeup in the Department Treasury occurred at this time, but further study is needed to determine if it was provoked by García Conde. Bloom, "New Mexico Under Mexican Administration," 2 (January 1915), pp. 242-45.

About the Author

David J. Weber is professor of history and chairman of the History Department at Southern Methodist University in Dallas. He is one of the leading authorities on the Southwestern United States and is author of 12 previous books including *Taos Trappers* (1971), *Foreigners in Their Native Land* (1973), *New Spain's Far Northern Frontier* (1979), *The Mexican Frontier, 1821-1846* (1982), and *Richard H. Kern: Expeditionary Artist in the Far Southwest* (1985).

Prof. Weber's work has won awards from such groups as the Organization of American Historians, the Western History Association, Westerners International, and the Texas Institute of Letters. He has served as a fellow of the American Council of Learned Societies, the National Endowment for the Humanities, the Huntington Library, and the Center for Advanced Study in the Behavioral Sciences at Stanford University.

With his wife Carol, Prof. Weber was named a Danforth Associate in recognition of bringing humane values to education.

And, he is one of the few North American scholars to have been elected to membership in the Mexican Academy of History.